The Faith Journey
of Impaired Pilgrims

Sarum College
31 March 2006

SARUM
College
PRESS

Published by Sarum College Press.

ISBN 0 9550660 2 6

Sarum College Press
19 The Close, Salisbury
Wiltshire SP1 2EE
01722 326899
bookshop@sarum.ac.uk
www.sarumcollegebookshop.co.uk

Contents

Introduction

A reflection on the weekend at Sarum College from which these papers, stories, poems and prayers come.
Donald Eadie

To set out for Salisbury was a faith journey in itself. From far and wide we came, from Darlington, Poole, Ipswich, Winchester, Birmingham and Southampton, tired, excited and nervous. We came with a variety of impairments, from different circumstances and from across the theological spectrum and different denominations. Five people in wheel chairs tried out the new lift and the blind found their way around unfamiliar corridors. There were spouses and carers, along with those working with issues of disability in local churches as well as at diocesan level, and also a large, strong yet gentle assistance dog. None of us had shared in an event of this nature before and we were all, staff included, learners. A unique community began to be formed.

Sarum College has a tradition of generous openness, a commitment to enabling theological exploration, and a willingness to learning from ancient and contemporary expressions of spirituality. Major building works have been completed including the installation of a new lift and hospitality can now be offered to people with a wide diversity of needs. Our invitation was to explore how the faith of people with impairments challenges the church, encourages individuals in their faith journey, and to model good practice for participants. The intention also was to address the needs of partners and carers whose lives are so profoundly affected by the impairment of loved ones.

We committed ourselves to listening.

We soon recognised that our shared process would require constant revision and an even greater priority had to be given to listening and learning from each other's stories. The thoughtfully prepared programme was quickly re-shaped.

Not many understand how our experience of our bodies has refashioned our faith journey. We need and want to be with those who do. We received from each other a new quality of attentive wisdom, empathy and insight. Our words reached a different level of honesty. Some spoke of their sense of isolation, desolation, loss of role and identity and abandonment by the traditional church, which offers sympathy and pity but doesn't know what to do with us.

We are told that we belong to a listening church but in general that is not our experience. People can't cope with how we are, can't live with not solving things; they want the healing that takes the problems away. The pressure on us is to recover and to return to so-called normality again. Imagine how it would be if time and space was made to ask how we really are? The church has yet to learn to listen for these pilgrimage of faith stories. How can safe spaces be set up for such listening?

Carers and spouses

We decided early on in the planning stage that the needs of the carers and spouses should be taken seriously. They would not be there simply to 'push the wheel chairs and chop up the food?' as one person implied. They also live with re-ordered lives and disappointment. They also are pilgrims with faith stories deserving attention. Often they are approached by kindly people inquiring after the well being of their disabled partner. Only the few ask, 'Your life has also changed, what is happening to you in all this?' And even fewer wait long enough to listen for an honest answer. Our weekend would make space for that listening

Healing?

'Jesus only healed a fraction of the people who came near him.' (Mary Grey)

Many of us have experienced hurt, even cruelty, from the church and in particular at the hands of those intent on healing the body. New wounds are inflicted at the level of our soul. The hidden pressure is to find the faith that leads to getting better, to physical recovery.

For some of us the issue is that of not being healed and being obliged to continue to live with chronic pain. Peter Cole, one such person, spoke of the tendency for 'uncured' disability to be something that we can't or won't think about. The miracle we pray for is to manage what at times feels unmanageable, to live wisely, positively, creatively and compassionately within the reality of our circumstances.

'We are learning that the church speaks much of pain and suffering but is embarrassed by it.' (1)

Where the faith journey can lead

Some of us are able to testify to the presence and providential care of God in our suffering. Others, however, find that our sense of God's presence in our lives and our previous belief in a loving ever watchful God, have been shattered. We understand why the disciples ran away on Good Friday. The faith journey of the impaired pilgrim often challenges the traditional view of God and God's world. This can be very threatening to other churchgoers and can also increase isolation. Where do we take the questions and doubts that can dominate and undermine faith for the impaired pilgrim?

We were reminded that theological and spiritual meaning can be found in our experience of our bodies, of being vulnerable, of being handed over. And more: 'Theology must not be left to those who are fit and strong. Theology must also be wrestled for through pain and disability: the raw material of our encounters with a mysterious God, whose name can seem to be hidden. That's how Jacob got his hip dislocated.' (1)

The continuing passion of God in the world is carried not in the abstract but in our human bodies and souls. I spoke of our slowness to make the connection between our limited, suffering bodies and the physical body of Christ.

Bearing the gifts of the kingdom in the world

'We see the sick as those being ministered to by the well, and fail to see how the sick also minister.' (1) What has to happen for the church to move beyond seeing the disabled as the recipients of ministry - to the discovery of the ministry of the disabled?

Mary Grey spoke of the two traditions of anointing with oil in the Bible. One is the anointing with oil for healing. And the other is the anointing with oil of kings, princes, priests and prophets in sending them out to use the gifts that God has given to them for good in the life of the world. It was this prophetic anointing with oil that was offered in the concluding Eucharist. We turned to each other seeking each other's forehead, the blind feeling for the face, the shaking hand steadied for the pouring out of the oil, and the murmuring of the words of blessing 'Go forth in the name of the Father to use your gifts in the kingdom.' Most of us have never been to a commissioning service such as this. We live within a new authority.

Some of us were reminded of Harry Morton, a former President of the Methodist Conference and also General Secretary of the British Council of Churches. It is said that after his stroke and during the years in Bow, only the brave came to visit and to stay with him in his broken attempts to communicate. On one occasion in his local church when it was Holy Communion his wheelchair was taken to the front and the plate with bread placed on his knees. Harry was unable to lift his arm enough to put the bread into the open hands of those who came. People picked up the bread and perhaps his lips moved enough to declare 'The body of Christ.' How, we wonder, can we arrange Holy Communions where the broken serve the so-called whole? (1)

We came to Sarum, listened, wept and laughed and then returned whence we came. We are learning and unlearning, fragile and resilient pilgrims on a faith journey. We are now interconnected, physically absent from each other yet also present for each other. We have been drawn more deeply into the mystery of the life and witness of the body of Christ.

In conclusion

Members of religious communities and people in many congregations promised to pray for us over that weekend at Sarum. And we are thankful. Before setting out on that journey to Salisbury one person wrote, 'To be at Sarum will be like being in heaven' and it was. She also added 'Will there be any guide dogs there?' And no doubt there will.

Donald Eadie

(1) An article entitled Disabled and Ministers published in the Church Times 03.03.0 is available from Donald Eadie donaldeadie@tiscali.co.uk

Keynote speakers

The Spiritual Journey of Impaired Pilgrims -
Mary Grey

Introduction

I'll start by trying to describe, sensitively, I hope, what it means today to be a believing Christian living with some degree of impairment/disability – aware of the huge range of conditions and challenges this covers, levels of gravity and levels of pain. Forgive me for certain sense of generalisation. Please also don't expect neat, polished answers. This weekend is about sharing our experiences and sharing our questions.

Most of us here have come to Sarum this weekend, with a deep sense of being marginalized and/or excluded – by both Church and society. Trying to come to terms with the fact that our levels of pain, the whole reality of our lives, seem to mean very little to the wider society, except as being objects of pity or special help. Yet we have a deep desire that our faith journeys are significant for the believing community. We yearn for a sense of recognition, inclusion and some meaningful belonging.

But, we realise - even those of us involved in Liberation Theology in varying contexts - that even activists for social justice don't put themes of disability and impairment high on their agenda. We live, surrounded by a society/Church with assumptions of normality that are exclusive – even if at the same time paying lip-service to Liberation theology that privileges all categories of the poor, vulnerable and discriminated against. It seems far easier to focus solely on economic categories of poverty abroad and ignore the colonising tendencies and patronising ways that

6

disability/ impairment/chronic pain are regarded here. That is, until it hits us personally - maybe ourselves, a terminal illness, a child's life threatened, a child born with a range of impairments, the early death of a partner, or simply the ongoing day-today task of caring for someone 24 hours a day. The truth is that most people keep these issues at a distance. And I want to look at the personal, social and structural reasons for doing this.

Let us first look at the personal reality of disability and chronic pain. Born with a disability/impairment, the chances are, unless you are someone like Diane De Vries, (her story is told in Nancy Eiesland's book, The Disabled God), who was born without arms or legs and who simply accepted that's how it is and rejected prosthetic limbs as artificial, the chances are that you spend your life trying to achieve the nearest proximity to the norms of normality accepted by society.

With the situation of chronic pain, (I have begun, personally, to understand a little of what this means during the last few months), the reality of pain forms your total horizon, restricts the contours of your life. Panic sets in when you realise this pain is here to stay. Maybe sometimes you wake up and for a few seconds you imagine that the pain has gone, and then the reality hits you – rather, the shock hits you, that this is how it will always be. Barriers are created between chronic pain sufferers and so-called normal people. People with some impairment or chronic illness are frequently regarded simply as objects of pity, needing only our sympathy and tolerance. Wheelchair users tell us so much about this: access is tolerated, even encouraged, but the experience of being talked-down-to is frequent. In society in general, the sense of being on the edge, even being hidden away, invisible, of never being able to match the norm, of clashing with the norm, is always present.

I remember when I lived in Belgium some years ago, trying to integrate a group of children with elderly women who had become classed as mentally challenged simply by long incarceration in a mental hospital, I discovered a large house isolated in the countryside. I had a strange intuition that something wrong was going on. I knocked at the door and discovered that it was a home run by religious sisters for blind, and mentally impaired children. My group's attempts to bring these children into our homes, trying to include them and give them new experiences, failed, because the sisters could only cope with the children if they were passive, and conformed to a routine of early bed and no excitement.

Chronic pain sufferers become boring to so-called normal people because illness is regarded as something that we should recover from. Take the antibiotic, swallow the pill and get better quickly is the norm. The analogy with dying is strong. When a loved one dies there is sympathy for maybe a fortnight, and then we are expected to brace up and get on with life. There is scant recognition of the need to start rebuilding and recreating your whole world in the contexts of both pain, bereavement and loss.

Faith responses

And what happens on the level of faith? On the level of individual reaction, the response is often, "O God, why have you done this to me?" I did exactly this when I found I had cancer some years ago. As if, first of all, that this is God-inflicted. For a purpose or a punishment. And of course, begging the question, "Why not me?" Why should I be spared what millions of women experience? So often the faith stories surrounding illness/impairment are of the ilk, "How I became a better person by living with this illness/ physical/mental challenge." God sent this to make me holy. It becomes part of the justification of suffering that is there to teach us to become holy. The "no pain, no gain" theology still prevails, as well as the idealising even ideologising of suffering, endurance, patience and humility. The biblical model of Job comes to mind.

8

The crux of the matter comes with the way suffering is associated with redemption. Here there is a further level of suffering in the way that, behind attitudes to healing, still lurks the sense that in the Bible sin is associated with illness/mental illness. This is still the case even if Jesus rejected the idea in John's Gospel, Ch. 9, in the story of the man born blind. When approached by the Jews, and asked, "Who has sinned, this man or his parents?" he replied, "Neither". Rather, the meaning lay in the way God's goodness might be revealed through him. Yet the idea not only still lurks but is very strong, that God wants healing from illness/impairment. The paralytic, the blind man, the deaf man, are all cured. Isaiah's prophecies are all about the blind seeing, the lame walking, water in the desert, all as sign of the Kingdom coming. They do not address the situation of not being healed, of continually living with impairment and pain.

An even more serious problem for faith is the way disability is used as a metaphor for weak and imperfect faith. We might want to call this the "I'm blind but now I see" syndrome. How often do you hear sermons on moral blindness? On being deaf to the voice of the Lord? Being deaf, or hard of hearing to the Gospel message? The last thing you want to hear when trying to live with a certain impairment or disability is for this to be used as a metaphor for deficient faith. This is paralleled by the situation in the Church of always being ministered to- and never ministering to.

Responses

So the question is, what can we do about all this: what kind of faith response is helpful?

1. Human Rights issues

For the last three decades there has been a considerable movement in the Human rights area. There is Disability Discrimination Legislation. Access to public buildings has greatly improved, facilities for the loop in Church – it is undeniable that there have been great changes, even if many of you here will point to great gaps and inadequacies. There are still far too many situations of disabled children being abused, of mentally-impaired people in care homes being victims of cruelty and neglect.

The second problem is that the underlying structures and norms for identity remain largely unchallenged.

2. Challenge models of normality

I want to suggest, first, that the whole model of normality is a social construction that props up the culture spawned by global capitalism. There is a long history to society's views. You could even look at it as a relic of imperialism and colonialism, recalling that colonised peoples used to be classed as degenerates, as sub-human. Sharon Betcher suggests that colonialism created a psychosocial map of "zones of degeneracy". The stigma of debility is associated with social spaces like slums. Think of the people rendered disabled by the trafficking in human organs in poor countries.

Secondly, Western capitalism nurtures the vision of the perfect body, kept in shape by constant diet of fashion, workouts, special foods and of course expensive clothes. What does not fit the norm must be marginalized. (In the USA 2/3 of people with disability are unemployed).

But, thirdly, faith structures play their part in keeping this model in place. Think of the way notions of "wholeness" govern the healing ministry – we all pray for a restoration of wholeness. Is it not a "wholeness" based on the ideal perfect body held up as the norm? Disability haunts and prevents the achieving of this norm, considered as a human right.

Thirdly, the prevailing model of Jesus is as healer, miracle-worker, and that of the Spirit is that of rescuing and repairing us from our broken bodies. In other words repudiating the human condition. Sharon Betcher again:

The metaphor of disablement has been used to establish over against it the physics of spirit as a terrestrially transcendent power.

What is the situation of those whom Jesus does not heal?

3. Challenge the models of healing and wholeness: how to re-image wholeness and healing is the question.

Re-read the Gospel: yes, Jesus as healer has been selected by many as the preferred model. The Jewish writer Geza Vermes describes Jesus as the prototype of the Galilean faith –healer. But there is another way to read the Gospels. When we read texts, think of the way we eliminate the senses. We have words before us, but cannot hear voices, touch or smell people. Jesus heard the cries of people in pain. It is their pain that has vanished from the text. Jesus only healed a fraction of the people who came near him. The stories of the pain-filled lives of countless others, people who were not healed, have vanished from the text.

Think again of the story of the paralytic, (Matthew 9).As a child I could never understand why Jesus seems to reluctant to cure him physically. I always wanted to ignore the interchange about forgiveness of sins and wanted Jesus to get on with what was really important. Why was the forgiveness of sins more important than the healing? What could the man have possible done anyway, in his impaired state? There is a mystery here as there is in Jesus's encounter with all sick/people with impairment. He shows compassion. He engages with the situation – but he seems to stress that being in right relation with God is the crucial point, more important than physical healing.

Change notions of vulnerability and dependency in favour of multiple models of what it means to be human, multiple models of flourishing. All human beings are vulnerable. With pain, with disability this vulnerability is very obvious, glaringly obvious. In the face of that I want to place the biblical truth, "We are created in the image of God," called, chosen and loved. Whatever bodily shape we are in. What others in their folly may shun, God loves.

Disability, impairment makes us dependent. But isn't independence a myth anyway? Money underpins the myth of independence - many people buy their way to the so-called good life. In the life of connectedness in the web of life, interdependence is the bedrock , the real truth.

Conclusion: The Wild duck image

I have a small image given to me by a group of women in the Grail Centre, Holland. We were all then recovering from some form of cancer. (One friend has since died). The duck was reminiscent of Ibsen's play, The Wild Duck. (In the play it is quite a complex symbol and crucial to the plot). But in the context of our group reflection, what was important was that the wild duck had been wounded (shot) and driven to the bottom of the lake, but it surfaced and carried on. Or was dragged up by the dog. You can choose your version! For me it is an image of wounded humanity - a glimpse of how we all are. Even if we sink to the bottom, even if we are struggling with the mud and the reeds, if only we can hang onto our determination to keep diving back to the surface and keep living to the fullness of which we are capable, whatever our condition. That's becoming, reflecting God's image. As one poet wrote: "This jack, this poor potsherd, is immortal diamond...". (Gerard Manley Hopkins)

Mary Grey

12

The Context of my Faith Journey,
Peter Cole

Introduction

I want to talk about my own faith journey of living with chronic pain. But I also want to draw on the experiences of many others who I interviewed, in the course of research, on the way the Methodist Church treats those with chronic pain.

My context is pain: physical pain, and the pain of being excluded, left out. My context is that I don't fit. The thorn in my side is also a thorn in the side of the church. I am a Methodist minister, ordained by a church that now struggles to find a space for my ministry or my story. My journey has become one of exclusion – not so much out of prejudice or malice – but out of confusion, lack of creative thinking, and fear of the dangerous truth I represent. My context is as one of the many who live in the uncomfortable and theologically challenging situation of those who are NOT healed.

We live in the space between Mark 1:29-34 and Luke 4:38-40: Both record the event in which Jesus heals Simon's mother-in law and then goes on to heal others who are sick. In Mark's earlier account it says, 'he healed many who suffered'. By the time Luke was writing that 'many' was theologically unacceptable and so was removed from the story. Also removed were the stories of those who WEREN'T healed. Their reality was ignored, excluded from the gospel story. Their memories are too dangerous, they don't fit. So in Luke's carefully spun version, ALL are healed by Jesus. How else could it be? How could a loving, powerful, healing saviour leave some still suffering? That's unthinkable. And so that is what it became, unthinkable: something we can't, or won't think about.

Perhaps Luke thought Mark had got it wrong. But I'm not so sure, because Mark's account IS the reality in which I, and so many others, live. Our continued suffering doesn't fit. Not in the technological story at the heart of our health system – which believes that all 'illness' can be cured, and which becomes puzzled and defensive when you don't get better! Or in the way the church structures its Ministry. Now Simon's mother-in-law, she fits perfectly! When ill, she is ministered to, and gets well. When well SHE gets up and ministers to others. That's how it SHOULD be. But that is not how it is, either for me, or for many others.

My Story

The context of my faith journey is physical pain, and the pain of exclusion. I live every day in some level of physical pain. Occasionally this becomes unbearable, but mostly it is just low grade pain, grinding on, all the time, exhausting and frustrating. I remain reasonably mobile but most activities, including sitting, standing, bending, etc, increase my pain.

In 1995, after struggling to minister under this burden of pain, I was 'guided' to the conclusion that full time Methodist ministry was no longer possible for me. I was so exhausted at the time that this came as something of a relief. Not so welcome was the gradual realisation that the church had no other realistic alternatives. Ordained ministry was either all, or nothing. For me, employed ministry of any kind would end. So I was 'retired' on health grounds aged 39. Unable to minister in the 'normal' way expected of ministers I was quietly excluded from all ministry. As was my reality and my story.

The Meaning of Pain: Loss and Disruption.

Pain has many meanings. My experience and my limited research suggest that the journey of pain often includes loss, exclusion and isolation.

Every sufferer is different, but pain frequently seems to threaten their world, their self identity, their story, and their understanding of God. This can be immensely challenging both to the pain sufferer, and to those around him or her. This includes the church community, both local and national. My experience is that the church doesn't handle this well!

i) Loss of World

Living with pain slowly affects your whole world. Pain becomes a constant boorish companion on the journey; it intrudes into everything, demanding attention, changing everything. Pain sufferers often have to stop work (as I did). They may lose financial security and the self confidence and sense of purpose gained from doing a job. Living with pain frequently involves a loss of activity. This can affect one's family and social life, indeed life in general! It can involve a slow movement from independence to dependence.

Pain can also disrupt your world view. Your world becomes a frightening place of contingency and chance: anything and everything could happen. It becomes a place of suffering and pain – your own pain and that of others'.

Pain can also deconstruct your world because it isolates. It breaks connection and it disrupts relation in at least 3 ways:

a) pain is private:

No one can truly know what YOUR pain feels like. It remains invisible, hidden. You can be standing next to someone and be completely ignorant of their pain. Not even love or deep friendship can break through this. Perhaps due to this private nature of pain, pain sufferers are often faced with disbelief. That fundamental, undeniable aspect of THEIR lives is doubted or questioned by others.

b) *pain breaks down language*

In extremes of pain – we can only cry out and pain is also notoriously difficult to describe. The only language that seems to work is the language of torture and damage.

c) *the story of continued pain is too painful to be told.*

When pain does not heal or reduce then gradually its reality becomes harder to share. After a while people don't want to hear your story because it just goes on and on with no conclusion. So you begin to hide this essential part of yourself, leading to increasing isolation. A barrier forms between you and everyone else, and relation and community become threatened. The pain sufferer's faith journey is often private and lonely.

ii) *Loss of Self and story*

Pain also disrupts the self. Torturers use pain for precisely this reason. Under its onslaught the kind, brave, loving person who might resist is destroyed. The everyday torture which their bodies inflict on those who live with chronic pain can also bring a similar loss of self. As we have seen there can be a loss of identity when work, activity, and social links are reduced. Loss of role in the family, community, or church can adversely affect your self identity. Living with continuous pain can bring a loss, or change, of character. The constant effort of dealing with pain is exhausting and leaves little energy left to 'be yourself'. People with chronic pain often suffer from depression and loss of purpose, hope and joy. They can become grumpy, short tempered and hard to live with (just ask my wife). Medication to relieve pain can often adversely affect personality. It can also become hard to lift your focus of attention away from the pain which intrudes and dominates your whole life. Also, as we have seen, pain tends to isolate. As we gain our self identity through our relationships, this too affects who we are.

So the journey through chronic pain often includes dealing with the loss of the person you were and the story you used to live.

iii) Loss of God

Interviews with church members in chronic pain were ambiguous. Some found that their experiences had brought them closer to God. They felt that God had been beside them in their suffering. Most of those I talked to however found that their continued daily battle with pain had destroyed both their sense of God's presence and their understanding of who or what God was. Their previous beliefs in a loving God who watched over them, cared for them, and was involved in their life had been shattered by their experience of pain. No-one expects to live a pain free life, but in the daily struggle with pain each moment seems an affront to idea of a loving God. This is often hardest on carers! They find themselves asking how God could do this to their loved one. They understand why the disciples ran away on Good Friday.

So the faith journey through chronic pain often involves challenges to the traditional view of God and God's world. This can be very threatening to other churchgoers and can also increase isolation. There seems to be nowhere to take the questions and doubts that can dominate and undermine faith for the pain sufferer. In these ways pain can threaten the loss of world, self, story, and God.

The Church's Response?

My experience and those I interviewed suggests that the church finds it very difficult to respond creatively to those who live with continuous pain. Why is this? The church is like everyone else. It finds it very hard to face the reality of such continued suffering. It finds it very hard to face the challenge such suffering brings to its models of healing and salvation, and it's understanding of a loving God. It also finds it very hard to face the challenges pain brings to its models of Ministry which assume that those who are not "well" are to be ministered TO! Such people are seldom seen as a valuable resource. Again and again I heard stories of people suffering with continuous pain who had gradually and quietly been excluded from church life. And this too is my experience. This is very sad because such people, precisely due to their difficult faith journeys, frequently have a great deal to offer.

Conclusion

Writing this has been difficult for we are taught not to talk about such things. We are encouraged to keep a stiff upper lip, to say we are fine even when we are not. In a sense this is at the root of the loss and exclusion described here. This is the point. I can't talk about the context of my faith journey without including such things. I AM someone in pain and living with the consequences of that pain – every day. To edit out the pain from my story is to remove part of who I am. Yet, as time goes on, sharing that part of the story becomes increasingly difficult. Even so, without apology, I offer this as the context of my faith journey and the context of the journeys of many, many others, including some of you.

My faith journey has been one of much loss. It needn't have been, but it has also become, a story of exclusion from established church ministry. My journey through pain has taken me to the margins, into the chaos and darkness at the edge of the church and the edge of theology and belief. But the more I tell my story, and hear the stories of those in a similar position, the more I realise that there seem to be a lot of us waiting, out here on the edge! Perhaps because, only in that chaos and on those margins, can take place the creative reconstruction necessary after so much loss. If so, it is a creative reconstruction needed by the whole church, not just those in pain, or those dealing with other forms of impairment. And I suspect it is a journey of reconstruction that will have to follow a similar path to that trodden by those dealing with pain: that is, a journey through the experience of loss and disruption of world, self, story, and even God. If I am right then those who live with pain may be able to offer to the church exactly what it needs. Their exclusion from ministry is therefore costly not just for them but for the whole church community.

Peter Cole

The Faith Journey of the Impaired Pilgrim –
Donald Eadie

1. I am glad to share these days with those who also experience our body as continually re-shaping our faith story.

Two things by way of introduction: I am free to explore the context and substance of our theme in the way I do because both Mary and Peter have first spoken in the way that they have done. The three of us live in different parts of the country, inhabit different worlds, yet in recent months have begun to work as a team and to compliment each other in our interdependence

And second- I know that I must not attempt to speak for my wife, Kerstin, and her faith journey through her early years in Sweden and through the 43 years lived in England. I do know, however, that the last 14 years has re-ordered her life as well as mine. Many continue to ask her, 'How is Donald? Are there signs of improvement?' And only the few ask: 'And how is all this affecting you? What of your faith journey?'

2. I want to speak of pilgrimage and of the beginnings of an exploration within 2 inter-related journeys.

But first, and briefly, something of my own context. An unexpected and unwelcome early retirement in 1996 was due to a developing degenerative disc disease in the spine. Three major operations have been necessary including the implanting of scaffolding.

The journey has also included moving away from the centre of the busyness of the Church into the borders, the margins and paradoxically coming nearer to the heart of things. Gerry Hughes once said to me 'The borders are the new centre, the place of discovery and of exploration.' The pilgrimage is lived within paradox:

- contraction and expansion,
- aloneness and belonging,
- apprehension and resolve,
- limitation and freedom
- physical pain, tiredness, and well being,
- weakness and resilience.
- blocked bowels, sickness and spring composts!
- dependence and interdependence,
- endings and beginnings,
- powerlessness and providence,
- the desire to control the future and also the willingness to be drawn into an unexpected to-morrow..

The world of paradox is not 'either/ or' but rather 'both and....' This is the terrain of pilgrimage. And contrary to all my fears there have been new companions for the way.

3. The first path leads into listening to and learning from our body

Some of us are slow and reluctant learners. In earlier years I was competitive in sport: cricket, hockey, football, squash, badminton, volley ball, tennis, table tennis, swimming, running, jogging and walking. In later years I worked long hours and travelled great distances in the car.

I continue to live with an inner motor, an inner drivenness that can be both creative and destructive. In moments of mindlessness I still push, punish, ill-treat my body. I continue to ask my body to do too much, to bear too much. And the journey includes a paradigm shift. There are voices around and within:

'You have a teacher, your own body. Listen to it and learn.'

'Learn body wisdom.'

'Take time with your body, learn the language of the body'

'Be gentle, be kind to your body.'

'Learn the story that your body can tell you.'

'You are what you eat.'

'Your calling includes being a good steward of your body'

'Learn the sacrament of the body and of touch.'

After my third operation the Anglican chaplain in the hospital offered the sacrament of the anointing of the body. In the Christian tradition from which I come this practice is not only unfamiliar, it has felt alien. This experience of the anointing of the body became part of the catharsis..

A friend who is a Roman Catholic nun has lived with rods in her spine for over 25 years. She offers spiritual direction to people from a lying position. During a visit to Bernie in hospital I noticed a sister from her own community sitting quietly at the end of the bed massaging her feet. When she left to go home Bernie grinned and said 'Foot massage is wonderful. I can recommend it and it also does such wonders for bowels that are slow to move!'

Bernie also introduced me to what it could mean to pray with and through the body. 'Every part of our body holds part of our story, a story with a past. Learn to listen and to learn from that story.' Both Bernie and I receive acupuncture from a person who provides not only skilled treatment but who is also a trained counsellor. He listens to the stories within our story. He gently nudges to where the connections could be. He reveres the wondrous mystery of the human body.

In her book 'Broken Body, Healing Spirit'. Mary Earle draws on the Benedictine tradition and in particular what is called Lectio Divina. She encourages a form of meditation that 'listens to the language of the body, tends the body, reads the body as sacred text.' The meditation includes focussing on each part of the body and adding the prayer: 'I will thank you that I am wondrously made' or 'I will thank you for the journey we have made together.' Mary Earle writes 'Learning to read the text of our bodies doesn't provide any magical cures. But it does give you a way to perceive presence within illness and to discover community in the process.'

I am learning that 'the body itself can be a hermitage when I have embraced it as quite simply the place where I know I shall meet God- the here and now of my actual humanity.' (source unknown.)

The first exploration leads into listening to and learning from our body.

4. And the second exploration makes connections between our bodies and our sharing in the life of the body of Christ, the passion of Christ.

I place this exploration in the context of a small group of nuns, priests and ministers in Birmingham who live with a variety of forms of disability

Our experience of limitation.
Some of us experience dependency on others for the toilet, for the washing not only of our feet but the whole body, for receiving food and drink, for being dressed and undressed. Most of us know something of being stripped, of nakedness and exposure, of being stripped of responsibilities, masks and dignity and of humiliation. We know something of pain bearing in its

different manifestations and also of abandonment and desolation.

We are learning that something creative can come out of limitation -and that something good can come out of the suffering. We are learning that theological and spiritual meaning can be found in our experience of our bodies, of being vulnerable, of being handed over.

These experiences can be the raw material of our encounter with a mysterious God, whose name seems sometimes hidden. And there can be rare glimpses of God in pain.

It doesn't feel like embodied incarnation, like being the body of Christ in the world. It doesn't feel as if the pain bearing belongs to a wider redemptive process nor that we are part of what Paul describes as ' completing what is lacking in Christ's affliction for the sake of the body, the church. (Colossians ch 1:24) nor ' that the life of Jesus may also be made visible in our bodies.' (2 Corinthians 4:10cf): We are daring to make the connection between our experience of our body, our limitation, our pain, our suffering and the suffering of the body of Christ.

The continuing passion of God in the world

A friend who is a South African nun speaks of the continuing passion of God in the world as being carried not in the abstract but in our human bodies and souls. She asks about the effect on our bodies and souls of our willingness to absorb evil, suffering, grief and shame willingly.

The mystery of interconnectedness

Attendance at our group meeting in Birmingham is affected by a variety of circumstances: intense pain, severe bouts of depression, a change of medication, or the illness of a carer – any of these can halve the attendance. How can those bodily present pay attention to the agenda of those bodily absent? How can we affirm our belonging, our communion with each other? We continue to live with these and many other questions.

The Eucharist speaks to us both of the mystery of the real presence of Christ in the sacramental bread and wine but also of the mystery of the real presence of Christ in all things, all circumstances and all people. The Eucharist also speaks to us of the communion of saints, the mystery of those whom we no longer see yet those with whom we are still together. We live within the paradox of absence and presence.

Much of what I have said will find resonance in the beautiful prayer that Peter has prepared for use in our closing worship. He has called it 'A communion prayer.'

Baptism into the Body of Christ

Kerstin's nephew in Sweden has cerebral palsy. He has never spoken, is unable to co-ordinate his movements and is totally dependent on others. He lives in a comfortable, life affirming and adventurous small community.

I baptised Jakob 32 years ago, placed the sign of the cross on his body. A few years ago he was confirmed into membership of the Church of Christ. This was not an assent to belief but rather an affirmation of the real presence of God in his body and the enrichment that he brings within his belonging to the marked body of Christ in the world.

Conclusion

Much of what I have said of pilgrimage and of the exploration of the body belongs to all human beings and not just impaired pilgrims. I close with a bread making prayer from Inderjit Bhogal:

> Lord bless the breaking of this bread,
> Bless the broken peoples of the world,
> Bless them and us and make of us signs of resurrection.

25

Broken Body, Healing Spirit by Mary Earle. Published by Moorehouse Publishing. A Continuum imprint.

Donald Eadie

The Communion Prayer for the Impairment Course – written by Peter Cole

God of mystery,
known through the crucified,
whose power refashions weakness and strength,
whose presence is embodied through brokenness,
we offer our awe and wonder.

With those who are broken by pain,
with those exhausted by the struggle to conform,
with those crippled by the insensitivity of others,
with those not seen as a resource but only as a concern,
we praise you saying,
Holy holy holy
God of vulnerability and love,
Heaven and Earth proclaim your glory,
Hosanna in the highest,
Blessed is he who reveals
the reality of God.

We bless the name of Jesus,
bone of our bone,
flesh of our flesh
whose brokenness and suffering make love real,
who on the night in which he was betrayed... etc.
Christ has died,
Christ is risen,
Christ redeems our stories.

Therefore as we eat this bread and drink this cup
we acknowledge brokenness as a path to truth.
We long for the bread of tomorrow:
eternally broken and so able to nourish.
We long for the new wine of the kingdom:
continuously poured out that thirst may be quenched.

Spirit of wisdom, brood over these bodily things
and make us one body with Christ
so that in the life of a changing church:
the broken may lead us towards wholeness,
the suffering show us the way to peace
and the excluded teach us of community,
so that all may receive
the gifts to be found
within the body of Christ. Amen.

The Experience of Presbyters and Deacons Living with Impairments, *Robin Hutt* *(Chair of the working party)*

Introduction

From "The Dream that Became a Nightmare for Mike Gregory" Interview with Dave Hadfield - Independent Wed. March 29th. 2006: (following an Employment Tribunal a week earlier).

"Mike Gregory, one of the finest Rugby League players of the 1980's had been head coach of Wigan when he developed what one specialist diagnosed as motor neurone disease, but others as progressive muscular atrophy caused by an infection triggered by an insect bite he suffered on a visit to Australia. As the condition developed Wigan Rugby Club removed him from the job he loved, though they honoured their contractural obligations by paying his salary until the contract expired. Gregory felt that he could have continued doing his coaching work for longer, and would himself have realised when he could no longer do the job properly, then for his own sake and for the sake of the players sake, he would have resigned. Gregory, now 41, was denied that option. The Disability Rights Commission, which backed his case at the employment tribunal, argues that, under the law as it now stands, he should have been given it."

The article ends with this paragraph:

" Wigan pointed out... that they 'had honoured every penny of our contractual obligation.' That, as far as the Gregorys are concerned, has never been the issue."

The issue - it seems to me - was about treating Mike Gregory as a person of integrity, enabling him to make his own decision about what he could do, and enabling him to do it. Loosing control over your own body I guess is bad enough, being deprived of the dignity of making your own decisions must make it even worse.

In the middle of the article is this statement: "In many ways Gregory's story has a resonance well beyond its sporting context. It is about how society in general and employers in particular, deal with serious illness and disability." I am going to say something of its resonances in the Methodist Church, but it may be that you will see parallels in your own experiences.

I was speaking earlier this week to a minister who had had to relinquish an inner city appointment that she loved and had hoped to continue in for the 5 years left before her retirement. However, the development of her MS meant she had to go to a less stressful appointment. Even that in the end proved too much and she had to retire early. She feels that she was treated well and with sensitivity by the church, not least, she thinks, because she had a very good District Chair - the pastoral equivalent of her bishop.

Sadly, her experience has not been shared by everyone in her position. For a long time a group of ministers whose experience has not been as good as it should have been, have been hammering of the doors of the church to ask that very serious consideration should be given to all the issues and implications that surround those who develop disabilities and impairments during the course of their ministry which significantly effected how they were able to work.

Then 4 years ago a door was opened, and 2 years later a report was submitted to the Methodist Conference entitled: Presbyters and Deacons Affected by Impairment. It outlined some of the problems, it contained some theological reflection, it suggested guidelines for good practice. and made some concrete proposals. Conference received the Report and instructed the

Methodist Council to set up a working party to take the issues further and report back.

The working party has met, its report will come before the Methodist Council, and if approved will be sent on to Conference this June - and the signs are that it will be. We hope then that Conference will discuss it, accept it and approve its far-reaching recommendations.

This whole process has been a shared journey and for many of us has involved a steep learning curve. I want to share something of our journey and what is in the report - though please understand that at this moment it is a proposal and not yet formally approved for action.

Getting going

It was crucial that people directly experiencing the pains and frustrations we were to consider should be part of the group. Those of us who had access to our strength and mobility were often moved as we became aware of the costs endured by those for whom getting to the meetings, spending half a day in hard work and facing a journey home was a massive effort. We were also aware for the frustrations of those who could not attend, and our own inadequate ways of involving them in the processes. We were all living the situation.

Starting points

When the church accepts a person as a candidate for training for the ordained ministry what we call a covenant relationship is entered into which includes mutual respect, care and support.

Therefore the understanding and support that Ministers who have to cope with impairments experience in the church must be at least as good as the best experience of people in secular employment.

Theological underpinnings

Although these theological statements are made in relation to people involved in the ordained ministry, I believe that they hold for everyone. You will find them on pages 6-8 of the Report. In summary they are first that we are all made in the image of God, who loves, rejoices in and anguishes over the whole creation. God has created diversity: it is at the very heart of the one we know as Father, Son and Holy Spirit, distinctly three and profoundly one. Therefore at the heart of God is a community of love, for love needs another to share it. Because God calls all people to share in that community of love, we should cherish, value, love, listen to and respect everyone as far as we are humanly able. So it is not surprising to see diversity reflected in those whom God calls to ordained ministry. This has clear implications for the way the Church responds to Ministers who have disabilities, for one aspect of diversity may be vulnerability and wounding. The uniquely Christian understanding of the nature of divine love, focused in the Cross, is where we see God sharing and taking into the Godhead all human pain and vulnerability in the broken body of Jesus Christ. The way the Church responds to the vocation and ministry of a person must reflect our understanding of the Cross and our belief in a vulnerable and wounded God.

Secondly, in 1 Corinthians 12 Paul makes it clear that the Spirit endows every child of God with gifts for mission. Ministers with disabilities are too often seen as bringing problems to be solved and as those who need pastoral care, rather than being seen firstly as people bringing gifts. Their gifts are rooted in the wholeness of their being as well as in the specific experience of their condition.

A third theological assumption is that a sense of call of vocation does not disappear with the onset of a potentially disabling illness or condition. Therefore one of the important tasks for the Minister and the Church is to work out together how best that person's vocation can continue to deepen, develop and be fulfilled, and their gifts used,

Visiting South Africa just before the dismantling of apartheid, people were asked if they thought it would ever come good. They said that they were Christian people. They believed in the cross, and saw echoes of it all around them. They also believed in the resurrection, which declared that goodness will overcome evil, that life will overcome death. Therefore they continued with the struggle. Because they did that the miracle happened. That is an example of the dynamic of true theology. There should be a similar dynamic in the theology outline in the report which we hope will result in the good practice the report goes on to propose.

Good practice

The guide to good practice includes:

People being affirmed as those whom God has called to ordained ministry and therefore the Church must do all in it can to enable ministers to fulfil their calling with as much flexibility and appropriate understanding as possible.

There must be good communication between church – minister and their family, friends and carers. All being encouraged to be open about the issues arising, confident of proper confidentiality being respected.

- Adequate training be provided for all the people mainly involved.

- Proper networks of support be set up and made available.

- Sources of relevant information should be made known and available.

Specific guidelines are suggested for different stages in the ministerial life: Candidature – stationing – ongoing ministry, especially in the movement from one appointment to another – retirement, especially early retirement if it becomes necessary.

The section on Good Practice ends with these paragraphs on page 15: " The presence of Ministers affected by impairment enriches the Church. We are called to live in the holy society of the whole wide diversity of God's people, and the more that ordained ministry reflects this, the richer the gift it is to the service of the Church. At all stages in ministry there needs to be awareness of the needs and understanding of the issues for those in ministry in such situations.

It should be assumed that Ministers will feel guilty, angry, traumatised – or indeed hopeful, defiant and upfront. These and many other feelings are stages and signposts on the journey of ministry by those so affected, but there should be openness in the procedures of the Church to enable any such feelings to be honoured, attended to and transformed as God gives grace through the Spirit."

There follows 9 clear and practical proposals to implement the spirit of the Guide.

It is good to know that alongside our work is the proposal that a Disability Justice Committee (parallel to our Racial Justice Committee) be set up in the Church, and there is funding available.

It is to our shame that we as a church have taken so long to get to this point. Those of us involved in the journey thus far have been enriched by it – despite its frustrations. I hope that at least some parts of this story have rung bells for you; and that you will feel free to feed in your responses.

Robin Hutt

Reflections from participants

Introduction

It has been a privilege to collect and edit these stories from the members of the course. Each person was invited to contribute and almost all did so although, as you will see, they responded in very different ways. I was not surprised at this, or by the fact that most threw away my carefully constructed suggestions and wrote from the heart. I am glad they did so for, as I hope you too will find, the stories that follow are powerful and often deeply moving. They challenge our easy assumptions about the experience of living with impairment, not least because they witness to the refusal to be categorised. I will therefore resist any attempt to offer generalisations except to say that I believe they all speak of the human desire to find meaning and hope in whatever life throws at us. I am humbled by their honesty and courage. P.J.C.

Eleanor Tew

One of the ways in which I first noticed my impairment in the context of my developing faith was at Sunday school. I was taught not to judge by appearances because that is not how God judges. This was not a very practical teaching for me with my very poor sight, as I had to learn to live among people who did judge by appearances without either treating this as a weakness on their part or begrudging the time and effort I had to spend in making myself and my surroundings look nice to please them.

My development was somewhat unbalanced when I left school. Although intellectually precocious I was in some ways ill prepared for the world, and I found my first year after school very hard. All sorts of things were happening to me which I did not understand. Looking back, I think that many of them were probably forms of discrimination against me as a woman and a blind person, but at the time I was not really aware of this. I looked for explanations and comfort in the Bible, but found little. The things that were happening to me did not seem readily comparable with what happened to disabled people in the Bible. This was part of the reason that my faith became so weak at that time. I had already accepted that I would probably never be cured, but had little idea of all the subtle and less subtle ways that people would find to treat me differently because of my disability.

I never regained the simple faith that I had experienced as a teenager and still have serious doubts about many aspects of traditional Christianity. However, having passed through a period when I was getting more spiritual nourishment from non-Christian sources than from Christian ones, I have in recent years returned to my roots. I feel at home in the tolerant atmosphere of the Quaker Meeting, where I feel accepted more than in most places. I have learnt that my reaction to the Bible as a disabled person was not unusual, and that disabled people in all faith traditions face discrimination and negative stereotypes, some more, some less. I believe that in this country the discrimination is getting less and the stereotypes are starting to be broken down, but there is still a very long way to go.

This was the context in which I attended the course at Sarum. From the first Friday evening session people from different denominations and with different disabilities, men and women, ordained and lay, mingled easily and a warm and supportive atmosphere soon developed. Participants had been asked to bring a symbol showing where they were in their faith journey with impairment, and were given a chance to put their symbol in the centre and talk about it. Symbols included a duck, which is always diving into muddy water and coming up again, and a beautiful glass cross with a bit broken off it. Participants listened attentively to one another and the session worked well as a means of drawing people together.

The Saturday morning session was about listening to one another's stories. For some people it was a new experience to have people listen to them without interrupting, and a few tears were shed. Someone asked me, "Is yours a listening church?", and I was able to reply with a little pride that it was. A major issue for a number of those present was that they had felt called to the ministry in their respective churches but not been able to continue the work for which they were ordained because of their impairment. The afternoon speaker described at length the steps now being taken in the Methodist church to address this by looking for practical ways to enable ordained men and women who become disabled to continue to serve. Someone said, "The churches are at last waking up to the fact that the Disability Discrimination Act applies to them". We also heard from people recently appointed as pastoral workers with special responsibility for difference and disability. It seems that there is a stirring of disability awareness in the churches, probably triggered by the Disability Discrimination Act. I had not realised that what is currently happening in Quaker Yearly Meeting is part of a wider Christian movement.

Sunday morning was largely spent in preparing and conducting an act of Eucharistic worship. We broke into groups to plan different parts of the service. There was not much talk of theology. Someone with a gluten intolerance asked, "Do I have to eat the bread?" We gave one another the kiss of peace, we each received the bread and wine from the person on our right and then offered them to the person on our left, (a new experience for many!) and we anointed one another with oil. In that service there were words and music and a little silence; there was confession and lament, hope and gratitude, giving and receiving – a wealth of emotion packed into an hour.

The conference, the first of its kind, was a success and may be repeated in other parts of the country. It was unusual among ecumenical events in that the coming together that took place was much more on an emotional than an intellectual level. Since then I have been sailing on Tenacious, one of the Jubilee Sailing Trust's tall ships. The weather was very bad and everybody was under strain, including me. I expected to be able to find my way round the ship fairly well, but this was not the case. I therefore needed more help than I expected and sometimes, especially when a lot of people were seasick, that help was not available. I was therefore unable to participate very much because I could not get to the right place fast enough or at all. Although there were some good moments in the voyage, my overriding impression was of being ignored, abandoned and apparently forgotten. On several occasions, for more or less understandable reasons, people just walked off and left me. The cumulative effect was to make me feel utterly worthless. I was quite shaken by this experience, especially as it contrasted so sharply with my expectations for a voyage on a ship designed to be crewed by equal numbers of disabled and non-disabled people.

Immediately afterwards I went to the Quaker Yearly Meeting in London and could hardly believe how kind people were. There was a special interest meeting on disability equality at the Quaker Yearly Meeting and it is hoped to set up a "listed informal group". I should like to be the contact for that group, but do not have suitable computer equipment at the moment. Maybe I shall be able to take over later. I want to learn spiritually from my experience, but it is still fairly early days.

Gerald and Sally Laws

Sally writes: At the time I was diagnosed with Multiple Sclerosis Gerald was retraining, from his work in the print trade, to be a driving instructor. He qualified a year later, in 1997, about the time I became reliant on a wheelchair for mobility. Many things in our lives together were changing all at the same time, but we coped with it as well as trying to maintain a normal home life for our children. Looking back we can now see what a difficult time it must have been for them, but we think they may be the stronger for it now.

My life was like many other Christians: moments on the mountaintop and plenty of days working away trying to follow my Lord in the valley. The diagnosis turned my world upside down. On the day I received it I went to a Local Preachers' meeting and found myself looking at a banner which said, "You are a new creation." 2 Cor. 5:17. Although I didn't fully understand it at the time, somehow I knew that this is what having MS would mean: God drawing me nearer to Him through my condition. This is indeed what is happening.

I have Primary Progressive MS and experienced a rapid deterioration for 18 months after my diagnosis followed by a period of stability, and then some slow, gradual improvement. Throughout all this I continued to teach RE in a selective, secondary girl's school. This wasn't easy. Having the support of a perceptive Headmistress, who could see that my teaching from a wheelchair improved the girl's perception of disability, helped me to carry on. I finally felt that the time was right for me to give up teaching in May 2005. My voice was giving me problems and I increasingly found that I could not project myself to the class over the whole school day. Following my retirement from school, I was determined not to 'vegetate', so I put what energy I had into preaching, youth group work and Local Preacher support. Needless to say I could do none of this without the constant support of Gerald, who can balance his working hours around my needs.

I now have all the equipment I need to make my life easier. I have learnt to manage my symptoms better. I have the practical and moral support of friends and colleagues, and I am supported by a great deal of prayer. It is hard to find words adequate to express my gratitude for this support. It enabled me, even at my blackest moments during two stays in hospital, to be aware of the everlasting arms beneath. Just knowing that I was loved that much had a tremendous healing effect and I take it as another confirmation of the indefinable power of prayer.

MS is a very variable disease. There have been times when I have wanted to turn over in bed and give up. But there have also been times when I have come to see having MS as a privilege in the sense of seeing life from a different perspective. I can speak with first-hand knowledge of being disabled and have tried to take a positive view of my life as it is now. Throughout my experience I have tried to face up to some searching questions. To the question of, "Why me?" I say, "Why not me?" On the dangerous issue of having enough faith to be healed I respond that my experience of healing is not a story of cure or success. I have not been cured, but I believe I am experiencing healing, there is an important difference. Cure is about endings, healing can be ongoing. I also believe that if we blindly seek the first, but are not open to the second, then we may be deeply disappointed and our faith in a loving God may be damaged. Somehow we need to find a balance between encouraging hope and having false expectations. I have experienced healing as the restoration of a sense of well-being. To me it means being able to live wholly, for health means wholeness and includes happiness. One cannot rush healing for frequently it doesn't come when we want it to or how we think it should. Healing is about waiting on the Lord. For me acceptance, though not resignation, has been a very important part of making sense of why things are the way they are. I pray that God will help me to avoid bitterness, resentment and denial.

My illness has been life changing. I have had to sacrifice my natural independence and become more reliant on other people. My condition has undoubtedly deteriorated and that is something I struggle with. Every time I find I can't do something I used to be able to do, I have a negative feeling in my stomach. I find it more and more difficult to maintain what I would consider as a normal lifestyle. My body experience has definitely slowed me down physically but has deepened my intellectual and spiritual experience. Pain and fatigue are big obstacles to what I would like to be able to do. So I am learning to live with MS: to live a very good, happy, full and fulfilling life. This has meant that I have had to learn the worth of being patient and to value the rest that I need. But I am pleased that I am still able to take some leadership roles in the church and that my faith has definitely been strengthened through having MS. I don't think striving after healing is God's way. I would rather thank God for the healing I have experienced and, in his strength, live as full a life as I can knowing my limitations and working with God towards further healing whatever shape and form that may take, whenever it may come, in this world or the next. I may have to cope with all kinds of symptoms now but I am convinced that at the end of this life there will be something glorious waiting for me. This is what I tried to convey at Sarum: that Gerald and I live for each day and enjoy life as much as we can.

To say that Sarum was a life changing experience for me seems overdramatic but it has made me think in different ways, and made me more determined to view my disability positively. Since having been at Sarum my call to preach has been strengthened. So what if I'm in a wheelchair! Other people preach with worse disabilities and surely what I have learnt through my disability is worth sharing with congregations? The extra free time I now have allows me to spend more time in prayer, Bible study and service preparation. As a local preacher I have the opportunity of sharing the Sarum experience with other preachers through the L.P. meeting. It was also very valuable to us to have time together to think about our relationship and the experience of impairment on our journey of life. The excitement of the first Sarum course could not be repeated, but the continuing sharing of so many experiences of impairment must be the way ahead to bring about the change of 'mindset' in the church.

Gerald writes: Life changing is exactly what happens when the role of the carer starts to dominate so much of 'normal' time. As Sally's condition has changed, my involvement with her everyday

40

life has increased and my own life has diminished. However you look at it that is a huge change as the balancing of time moves from one focus to another. I sometimes wonder what life might have been like now if Sally did not have MS. But it can only be a dream as no one can predict the future with any accuracy or certainty. We still make plans for the days ahead, except now the timescale is a little shorter and the expectations a little lower. That's not to say we are planning less, we are just more realistic with our horizons.

The mysteries of MS have haunted me ever since Sally's diagnosis. At the time I tried to reason why one person should develop an illness and the next person is healthy. It frightens me that all of medical science cannot pinpoint the cause of this illness. It suggests that the human body is a fantastic, yet still mysterious, organism beyond the complete understanding and control of humanity. As Sally's condition changes, I change my response to her 'body needs' and over the years I have had to accept that the changes are always negative and subtractive. They always require more of my time and patience, as well as Sally's determination to not let these things of the body dominate the things of the soul.

Keith Hallett

I was born with cerebral palsy and epilepsy. The medical treatment I was given by physiotherapists and speech therapists at school in Bradford enabled me gain reasonable skill levels with my damaged right side although I did have slurred speech until aged 7 and even now my speech can be affected in this way when I am tired. My epilepsy is controlled with medication. The enlightened thinking, particularly of my head teacher, has enabled me to look beyond my impairments to such an extent that I do not first and foremost consider myself to be disabled. I am who I am.

I was invited to become involved, as a youngster, in my local Methodist Church but did the usual teenage thing of opting out.

This lasted for a year and then the Sunday school teacher invited me to join Central Hall in Bradford where I eventually became a member. Over the years I received encouragement from Ministers and lay people. I was employed by the Bradford Education Committee as a peripatetic gardener. I moved to the West Country having met my future wife, Margaret, at a house party at Cliff College. She was visiting Cliff with a party from the West Country. I transferred to the Housing Department in Bristol as a caretaker in 1966.

My call to preach came about when I was asked to take a service at Farrington Gurney Methodist Church when the planned preacher failed to turn up. After this the words of W. E. Sangster kept going through my mind "You tell them about Jesus, don't just leave it to the ordained." My preaching journey had begun. I became accredited in 1971.

Coping with my own impairments has made me more attuned to the fact that not everyone with disabilities, or their families, wants to share their problems. We must be sensitive: listening to those who wish to share but not expecting everyone to do so. Also it does help if you have a sense of humour!

With regard to my faith: I feel that we need to look afresh at the use of stock answers when it comes to whole areas of Biblical thought on disability. We need to use fresh ways of expressing this issue. Preachers who do not have a personal knowledge of impairments need to get alongside those who have. We need to look at things "outside the box" of the church. We have to be engaging with a theology of disability. My understanding of God is reflected in Jesus. He identified with people on the margins. He broke with convention. God's love is for all.

Living in a rural environment and not being able to drive means that not only is public transport very important but I also have to rely on other people being aware of my need for transport so that I can attend events, services, and meetings. I have to say that

I am now fed up with having to ask for lifts. I feel that churches/circuits should be more aware of this issue. Over the years I have received encouragement from teachers, Ministers, lay people and at the moment I have found belonging to a Ministers' fraternal at Downside Abbey very helpful. I enjoy collaborating with others and have been working with my own superintendent to give insights on disability issues.

After the course I can see that there is a move towards "joined up thinking", a feeling of sensitivity and discernment – keeping private what needs to be kept private. With regard to future developments at Sarum I would welcome the development of the following:

A theology of disability alongside the teachings of Jesus.

Exploration of faith journey experiences.

Addressing the environment: when a new building is planned we should look at accessibility. Making people welcome. God should be accessible to all.

Fresh expressions of theological training.

Challenges to ministerial training.

An accessible gospel that applies to all.

Susi Burdell

As a nurse, hospitals were not unfamiliar places but as Susi waited for her own MRI brain scan; professional confidence had been stripped away and neatly folded into a basket along with her clothes. As a patient, the hospital felt overly clinical, devoid of emotional response. Lying on her back with her head secured in a white plastic frame, the scan's tunnel seemed claustrophobic and imposing. Time passed slowly in this isolated compact space. She allowed the intermittent pneumatic drill-like vibrations to unearth her fear and cried with pools of tears collecting in her ears. In the year of this first brain scan Susi had been 29. Up to that point life had been vibrant, multicultural and taken at speed. She knew what it was to fall in love and plan the names of her children.

"I am afraid you are going nowhere", said the neurologist from behind the scaffolding of case notes. Susi heard the words but, having allowed her mind and emotions to already board the plane to Sudan, she was having difficulty accepting their impact. Back at home, Susi relayed this news to friends, family and the missions board, with her usual outward buoyancy. Inwardly God had pulled the plug on her soul. "How can you do that?" Susi said as the gridlock of anger numbed her prayers. "How can you pluck my life from atheism, fuel in me a passion for the persecuted church, train and focus my perspective around long-term service abroad, let me leave my job and sell my belongings, speak to me in prophetic language from different people over a period of ten years only, at the final hour, to tell me I can't go?.........How can you do that?"

Others found this level of uncertainty unsettling: the periscope of their faith overshadowed by a towering vulnerability which was unregistered by the radar of daily worship. If this could happen to Susi, perhaps it could happen to them? Explanations were necessary, which individuals gave, before turning purposefully away leaving Susi to float alone: "You obviously had some hidden sin. That is why this has happened". "Well, you were never meant to go in the first place, were you?" "Have you ever tried praying the Lord's Prayer this way?" Even treatment and therapy came under fire. "Why do you bother with physiotherapy? Surely you just need more faith?"

It was Sunday morning and Susi drove out of the car park just as others jostled to drive in. She could not bring herself to go into the church. Her emotional defences had been vandalised. The voices that crushed her were few in number but they sought her out, unaware of the damage being inflicted. Had she needed more faith? Her life had been witness to much impairment in her own body and in others, but she struggled theologically to associate this with a lack of either faith or strength. Surely weakness and faith co-exist?

Later Susi lay on her bed. Her eyes, though closed, danced with images from the lives of people from her past - now interwoven and allowed to form an integral part of Susi's understanding of loss. Drifting in and out of sleep, her mind sifting through her life, she allowed herself to be transported back. She found herself once again looking out from the small window of a noisy plane juddering through air pockets over the mountains of Zhob. Working in a hospital nestling within the North West Frontier Province of the Pakistan/Afghanistan border introduced Susi to issues of impairment, suffering and faith that merged with the dinosaurs of poverty, oppression, mass displacement and war.

Lying in Susi's arms was three-week old Mungpulli ('Peanut', because of his low birth weight) his little body arched, rigid with tetanus. His own mother was already dead and his life hung in the balance. The two had little in common but a strong bond developed. Then there was Fazia, with a mouth full of polystyrene packaging - because her grandmother thought that anything coming from the pharmacy had medicinal qualities.

Other countries held other memories. Sharing a traditional Czech meal with a quiet middle aged pastor who described how he had climbed out of the first floor window to our right, to flee the authorities, his Bible study materials sewn into his mattress. When caught he was taken for interrogation. Hutschenhausen: and Briggita who had been slashed twice across her face, leaving aggressive crocodile scars, whilst each wrist was decorated with friction burns from being tied to a radiator during the GDR system operating in Eastern Germany. She embraced Susi and asked her to pray with her. Yesterday Briggita had given her life to Christ. Today she brought to Him her brain tumour and her unborn child. Then there was Moses from Ethiopia who sat with his disabled wife explaining how he had been placed naked over a barrel, then had the soles of his feet whipped with canes. "I couldn't do it, Susi", he said. "How could I renounce Christ? He is my very breath". Finally, back in the U.K. Susi listened to people like Sally, a young, single mum, with a four month prognosis and an over-active five-year old. So traumatised was she by this prospect that she could only recount her story to an interested Jack Russell. People had not known how to reach her. Bonnie simply held her gaze.

Susi remembered her first encounter with Yahweh, the God of the bible. As an atheist, having realised that prayer was the aorta of the Christian faith, she decided to demonstrate to her Christian friends why their faith held no substance for her, and so end their persistence. She voiced the question, "To the Father of Jesus Christ in the history books, where are you in this world?" Yet it was not a question and was by no means intended as an invitation. It was rather her statement made in utter confidence that there would be no reply. But a palpable 'otherness' completely enveloped her. So impacting was this intimacy that she cried out, "Have my life. Do with it what you will. I am so very sorry". The safety of this relationship invoked the haven of both powerlessness and trust.

Ten years on Susi was in need of finding a human being with whom she could be this honest. Her fear was not that God no longer existed, but that she could not follow Christ with integrity. The routines of church life felt shallow and activity-driven. Was she losing her faith as some implied? She could no longer find a foothold. Barbara, a religious sister, allowed Susi to sob, to pause when the words could not be found and to admit to all that she had become, without judgment. She took time, listened and responded when the story had been told. "Susi, I don't think you are losing anything, let alone your faith, but rather experiencing brokenness", she said.

Susi then walked in the orchard, walking stick carefully placed so as not to lose its grip. "If I really describe myself today Lord I am this leaf, dried to a crisp, curled and devoid of moisture". Walking back down the slope to shelter from the wind, Susi heard the voice that had been so absent: "If that is how you are feeling", the Lord said, "Then notice how you are holding the leaf." Susi's hand clasped around the leaf in an open claw, allowing it to rattle furiously, but safely, with every gust.

Now, 41 years old, Susi is a full-time powered wheelchair user. She reflects on how her own inner storm has at last passed. Although a professional, when sitting with pain in herself or in others by way of counselling, Susi knows that each person will continue to have the need for an open dialogue about faith – their finding it, wrestling with it or their loss of it. Such people may be opening their hands and allowing dementia to gradually dissipate their identity; or walking into the hospice side room, knowing that they will leave in a metal box, and trying to prepare their children for their death. Susi has learned that most of us are just at the starting point of this journey, whether professional or client, nurse or patient, minister or member.

Here in the midst of impairment, loss and pain Susi finds Christ creatively at work, and she whispers, "I am under vows to you. I am the Japanese house made of paper. You, like a hurricane, lay me to waste. Here in my brokenness everything changes but you. How can I dare to believe? I wake from this dream to see you walk beside me, and all that I see is you. I just want to be with you, impossibly beautiful, but beautifully true." (From Daniel Goodman's 'Impossibly Beautiful, Note for a Child'.)

Joyce and Peter Berry

Disability has changed my life a lot, such as not being able to go out on my own, and relying on other people to do things. I am not house-proud but I like a nice clean home. Sometimes I think I have done things properly but I haven't, so somebody else has to do them. Another frustration is shopping. You've got a shopping list, you go to the supermarket but you can't see what there is and so you just get the same thing each week. Another thing I mind is having to bite your tongue before you speak sometimes. For example, when you go out some evenings you just sit there. People come and say hello to you but you feel so alone, and people treat you as if you are mentally handicapped just because you can't see. Some people can't put up with disability. We have lost so many friends. I get upset very easily, and often feel down when I think I could do things better. But then I think, well it's meant to be, so stop worrying and get on with it. Other people are worse off than me. I can go out, I can do things, but a lot of people can't.

What has the church done for me? Not much really. We go on a Sunday and there are lots of lovely people there who come and greet you, hug you and kiss you sometimes, because it is a friendly church. But now we have got a new vicar. He's changed everything. Like the other Sunday when he brought a table right into the centre of the church for communion. When it was time for communion we did not know what to do. Some were going to the right, some to the left. I didn't know where to go for the bread or the wine. When you go on a Sunday you are hoping for a bit more, I would say, 'religion', such as talking more about the Bible. But they don't seem to bring that in nowadays. You have the gospel readings, and they are very nice to listen to. But when we come home we say to each other, 'What have we learnt today? Not much at all! So why did we go?' I would like to move on a bit more, learn a bit more. But when you can't read it is so difficult. And people who read the Bible in church – often I can't even hear what they're saying. So we enjoy going to church, but we wish it meant a lot more to us.

The church people knew we were going to Salisbury for the conference on disability and faith. But not one person has asked us what we learnt, or what we have brought back to our own church. They are just not interested. If we try and say anything they say, 'Oh yes', and that is it. They just don't seem to want to know any more about it. We've been waiting for a loop system, and we've now got one, but it never works properly. We've got people that are blind and deaf, deaf people, and old people who would simply like to hear more – such as when the little children take part in the service. But most of us can't sing because we haven't got words to read from. And that is one of the hardest things I have found. Peter and I belong to the PCC and have always loved doing the gardening at church. But now we've been told we can't do it anymore despite doing it for many years and getting good responses. I love cutting trees down! Peter just stands me against them with all the tools and says, 'That wants to come down'. I love it! But now it has all stopped until somebody decides what they want to do and whether to include Peter and me to do it. This hurts both of us.

Where is my life journey going? I don't know really. Something needs to change, but I'm not sure what. I don't know where to pray. We've been to the Catholic Church, to a healing service, and that is very nice. The Sisters have encouraged us to go to one of the old people's homes on a Wednesday and so we will. I hope it may give some different meaning to life. Any suggestions for a blind person about the religious side of life would be very welcome.

What encouragement have I had since I have gone blind? Well, I had a social worker come three years ago and she helped me to read, 'Moon' (a simplified Braille). This has been very useful. I can have library books now, although they are about 8 x 12 inches, and in 13 volumes! The postman comes with all these parcels. And I'm sure he's thinking, not her again wanting more library books, doesn't she have enough! We have asked about having sections of the Bible. But no, that is too many. But I am very grateful that she has taught me to read. Now I am learning

Braille and that is very hard. I don't think I will ever be able to read a whole book properly. But I will take my time and, maybe one day I will. The Guide Dog people think I am a good candidate for having a dog but that would mean more to learn! They have told me I have got to learn how to use my cane first so that I can go out on my own. But the family says I am not to go out on my own! So what happens is that Peter goes out with me, he stays right back, but is there with me if I do make a mistake.

My hopes have changed a lot, because I could have done more to help people. It has altered a lot, but I hope I do give people more help when they come to the church. One old lady said she had missed church for two weeks because she was so tearful and thought she had better not come. I gave her a hug and said to her, 'I'm here anytime if you want to talk'. And she said to me, 'Why is it that I can always talk to you?' This is the kind of thing I like to hear from other people! I don't mind listening to them and I hope to give the right answers.

When we came to Salisbury for the weekend conference both Peter and I found it very, very useful. The people there accepted us, even though we didn't know anyone. It was really nice. And we could communicate with other people with disabilities. Everybody just spoke how they felt, and how uplifting it was to listen to some of those people. Trust me to be tearful again, and find I couldn't speak! But when people are so nice to you I do seem to get tearful. Peter felt it was very useful especially when we went into smaller groups and Peter joined the carers group. It's nice for him to speak to other people and to get things off his chest because he is such a private man and he doesn't speak very often. He sort of bottles things up and doesn't like to see me like this. But that's just one of those things. I look after him when he is in a lot of pain. We just get on with it and help each other and we make a life for ourselves that his happy. And we think the same and do the same things. We have recently started blind and

50

partially sighted ballroom dancing and they are lovely nice teachers. We get on so well together. I go to the Salvation Army once a fortnight and they are so nice to me. They have said that they have never had a blind person to teach or to look after. I am their guinea pig and they do look after me so well. Peter goes to his deaf club. He finds it useful as it gets him out of the house and he can talk to other people without me being there. I think that you need this little break now and again. We both go to 'Sailability' now and they agreed that we could be in different boats and let each other do what we want and enjoy ourselves. They are a lovely crowd of people. So that has altered our lives. We do get out a bit more. So, what can I say? Just thanks for our health and happiness.

This tape is all mixed up I know! But please put it into words that you want people to read about. Thank you again to everyone because you made us so welcome at Salisbury.

Barbara Houston

In December 2002, I became paralysed from the waist down, due to an attack on my spinal cord. I spent 2 months in a rehabilitation unit, learning to adjust to life in a wheelchair. In April 2003, my father died unexpectedly, and 7 months later, my mother passed away, also unexpectedly. I felt that life was pretty unfair, but I had to learn to live with it.

At our work's Christmas meal that year I had an interesting conversation with my job share partner, who happens to be a Methodist lay preacher. I questioned what life was really all about, and how unfair it all seemed to me. Anyway, to cut a long story short, I ended up deciding to 'try out' the local churches. My husband Barrie, who has been extremely supportive, agreed to accompany me. A few weeks later, we heard about an Alpha course, which we decided to 'give a go'. I have to admit, I was rather sceptical. Having been brought up in an atheist household I was having real difficulty with Christianity. However, about halfway through the course, I had an amazing experience at the Sunday Service. The sermon seemed to have been written just for me – the message was so clear. And then, during the hymn, I felt my heart start to race, and I was overcome with emotion. I felt that I had received the Holy Spirit. I approached the remainder of the Alpha course with a very different attitude, and declared myself a Christian.

Life trundled along well for a while, and I felt 'whole', despite my disability. However, 2005 became quite a challenging year. In February I became further disabled, following another attack on my spinal cord this time in my neck, meaning my arms were affected. I had to spend a further 2 months in rehab. However, my faith kept me strong – I was even confirmed into the Methodist Church that Easter.

I felt able to return to work at the beginning of May, but my employers disagreed. A long battle ensued and my faith began to wobble. What had I done to deserve such problems? I had given myself over to Christ so why was I being punished? I was becoming increasingly frustrated by my disability and with society's ignorance towards disability. However, I then had a further transformation, and decided that I was strong enough to fight not just my own corner, but that of others. Perhaps that was what was intended for me. Michelle, my Christian job share partner, spoke to me at length regarding 'God's Plans'. Was this God's plan for me? I began campaigning locally regarding poor parking facilities and access to services. I was also on a personal campaign to get back to work. My fight to return to work took several months to resolve, but I got there in the end. Some improvements have also been made locally for the benefit of others.

Then came the weekend at Sarum. What a wonderful experience. It was so humbling to meet with others, and share stories. Everyone there had an amazing story to tell. I no longer felt alone. Even more spiritual was our re-encounter with Donald and Kirsten, whom we had met some 18 months beforehand on a plane back from Cyprus. We had been sat next to Donald on the plane, and spent time talking to him and his family. We never knew their names, but for some reason they remained firmly embedded in our thoughts. When we met them again at Sarum that weekend, it was truly incredible – it must have been another of God's plans!

I came away from that weekend very inspired. I was once again on a campaign, this time wanting to ensure that the churches in my circuit were fully inclusive of all disabilities. This has not been an easy task, and I have met with a somewhat negative response. However, I am determined to persevere, and I will not let it drop. I have the determination and ability to help others, and that is what I will do!

Nonetheless, my faith has been challenged again this year, as I had a stroke in May. Once again I asked 'Why me?' Haven't I had enough to contend with? The answer of course is 'No'. Following all my medical setbacks, good has come from it, in a range of ways. I am a much more assertive person following all this, but I can also empathise with others. My faith has grown tremendously, particularly as I only learned of God just two years ago.

In our circuit newsletter, I noticed an advertisement for a District Disability Officer. This is too huge for me, but anyway the post has already been filled. Nonetheless, I have decided to contact the District Secretary, to suggest I could possibly be of support to this officer, in a different capacity, as he is blind and I am wheelchair dependent, so it could be looked at from two different perspectives. Alternatively, my thought has been that the District is a very large area. It might be more effective to have the District Disability Officer act as co-coordinator to more local disability representatives – perhaps two or three circuits being covered by the local officers

Would I have achieved all this had I not been an impaired pilgrim? I strongly believe none of this would have been even conceived by me without either my disability or my faith.

Margaret Oxenham

Being 'called by God' and accepted for Ordination by the Methodist Church at the 1993 Conference was something I never thought could happen. Why? Because I had never sought this gift and also during the previous year I had suddenly found it impossible to walk in a straight line; lift heavy objects or stand still without falling over if I had no support to lean on.

My condition was uncertain. Things like MS MN and ME had been mentioned, but no diagnosis was confirmed and I was ordained and made a Junior Supernumerary all within the space of a few days. The six Churches in the Circuit over which I had pastoral oversight were so supportive, and so was The Methodist Church system.

I moved to a MMHS bungalow close to my family near Salisbury and set about rebuilding my life as 'retired due to ill-health' after only 18 months in Circuit. The rest certainly helped and within a year I was out of the wheelchair, and off the walking frame. The diagnosis of Proximal Myopathy of unsure origin was made, and it was suggested that if this had been due to a virus I might eventually be free from it forever.

The Methodist Church re-instated me and I was sent to the Cornwall District where I served for 8 years with pastoral oversight of 6 churches (many of the members living up 60 or more steps to their front door!). Eventually the time came to move on and I was given the impression that I could quite easily cope with a Superintendent's job. I did not tick the little box on the Stationing Form but when asked to look at an appointment, I must admit I felt obliged to do so seeing The Church had been so supportive of me. After just a year I knew the workload was taking its toll, and I applied to the Stationing Advisory Panel to look for a different style of Ministry due to my health problems. By now I was walking with great difficulty using a stick. Climbing stairs was becoming impossible, and I was sitting to take all services. But I did not have any time off (my own decision). I felt scared as I could see myself back in a wheelchair and having to retire yet again.

I did not feel that my conversations with the Stationing Advisory Committee proved helpful. I felt I had entered the Headmasters Study only to be told it was all my fault! To be fair I do acknowledge that I was working long hours and this does cause my muscle condition to react adversely. I was told, 'Just stay put, don't do anything, and if the Circuit goes under, it goes under!' This certainly did not help as I was feeling guilty enough. I left in tears deciding I would look for a different form of ministry which would be less physical. The Panel agreed to this.

I worked for a year as a Hospice Chaplain, and although this was rewarding I knew my gifts were not being fully utilized. I applied to re-enter full-time Circuit Ministry on the understanding that I would not be a 'Superintendent' and that I would have a small appointment. This was agreed and I take up my new appointment in September 2006: nine churches in a very rural part of Cornwall! I am looking forward to my appointment as I have always worked in Rural Methodism.

I am concerned about the amount of ill-health and disability which has overtaken so many of my colleagues .Also the seeming lack of concern when these people have to 're-route' their Calling. Not many years ago Conference acknowledged a paper on 'Flexibility in Ministry.' .This talked strongly of supporting differing styles of Ordained Ministry, and of recognising the call of people from all spheres.

Attending the 3 days at Sarum made me realise that my health problems were nothing compared to others; and that many had gifts and talents that could be used whatever their physical abilities .We are confronted by a lack of ordained clergy, yet here is a band of people just waiting to be acknowledged and accepted. It will of course mean changes such as offering smaller appointments; changing the style of Manse; or accommodating a Minister who needs to sit 99% of the time. But God does not see the Disability, he sees the Possibility. How I pray the Methodist Church will learn to do the same.

Beth Sharratt

The title of the course spoke directly to me. I came as a Sister in a nursing home, a hospital chaplaincy volunteer, and as myself. A human being, who is imperfect, damaged, struggling, and who nowadays knows deep joy and deep pain. In nursing I have known a good many who have lost much (mobility, speech, control of bodily functions, sight and hearing), but who are whole. Amidst their pain and frustration, which do at times need to be expressed, they shine through. It is a privilege to know them.

In hospital chaplaincy my underlying view is that I, who am sick, visit you who are sick if you will allow me. I respect you as a whole human being, a child of God. I meet God as I encounter you. You minister to me through your strengths and in your need. I feel it is a joy to be alongside people of all faiths and none. And I want no over confident Christian who is 'well' to ever visit me to put me right! I have been challenged by the belief that it is not our usefulness but who we are that counts. Can I learn to be me? A unique, imperfect child of God, his creature, loved and forgiven by him, and responding thankfully to his ongoing suffering love? We resist being stripped, we resist 'failure'. Thank God for showing us himself in the stripped and apparently failing Jesus. We need to let go of much – including false religion. I have known people who are whole yet who have been stripped of almost everything. I have seen people die thus.

I was brought up in a deeply unhappy Christian home by parents who preached, taught and understood the various Greek and Hebrew meanings of love, but who were unable to express it. (My heart, now, at long last, goes out to them.) I nevertheless absorbed faith through church teaching and good 'ordinary' souls in the church and chose it for myself. My parents always disagreed, so everything I did as a child was wrong! This of course caused deep seated low self-esteem.

An unhappy person, I resentfully went into nursing rather than music (my obvious gift and love). I succeeded, becoming a kind, caring and skilled nurse, but I knew a deep inner unhappiness. Two good churches held and sustained me. When ill in my twenties a Christian colleague said, "You know God loves you." I responded flatly, "Yes, and what is love?" I had a good husband and three lovely boys but was not happy. Loss of career through family commitments led to clear midlife crisis at forty. The ongoing low self-esteem led to self-rejection and rejection of those closest to me. I isolated myself and became desperate.

By now I had stopped attending my local church because I felt there was no opportunity to be real. This was only partly correct. I suppose I should have tried but I was in no state to open up. Then in 1994 there was a turning point when a new minister came who chose to visit non-attenders. I was receptive and appreciative and clearly had a spiritual hunger. He had no idea I had NO visitors or that there was anything wrong, but he visited quarterly even though I did not return to church. On the fourth visit I broke down declaring, "My life is a mess. Why do you bother? Why do you visit me?" Quietly he replied, "I visit as a sign of God's love" This rang true. I knew in my heart for the first time that God's love had touched me and that actually it had long been doing so. It was as though a veil (of forty three years) had been removed. Wow! So this is love: God's persistent search to find the way and the moment to show his on-going concern. I realised in my heart what I had believed in my head: that God had been alongside me and loved even me. Today I realise how often simple human touch and care can enable someone to discover, receive and respond to God's love. Looking back it seems my early struggles have made me sensitive to others' pain. This showed in nursing when I saw each patient as a human being, and challenged others to do the same.

I returned to church and came out of my shell. Within a week I enjoyed visiting the housebound and went into my son's primary school. I listened to children's reading, building up the confidence of some who struggled. I soon found kids greeting me cheerfully in the street. It was a shock to realise how much I'd been opting out. I immediately stopped rejecting those closest to me. I began to rebuild relationships using the resources I had been given. I knew inner joy, peace, contentment. I no longer reacted negatively within the family. Today we continue to work at our marriage as everyone must. We are glad to be doing so.

The week following the turning point I joined the Bible fellowship. We studied John's Gospel. It spoke to us for two and a half years. The few who came were deeply challenged by its message. Soon I was leading it for long periods because the minister was very unwell. It seemed there was a hand in all of this. Within the group, or as leader drawing others out, I had a deep hunger and excitement. It was catching. I realised that my enthusiasm for hearing the bible was helping me grow and that this had to be shared. So I began the process of testing a 'call to preach' which I'd heard two weeks after my return and which had seemed such a nonsense for a recluse! I can now say that preaching is a BLESSED nuisance! Sadly, within this joy, there is much church pain. I have seen and do see inappropriate power struggles and panic attempts to make the church successful. For me the way forward is not to try and reinvent the church, or God, but to have deep roots; to encourage others to put down deep roots; and to be alongside others as a sign of God's presence and love. Most of that must be done by being the church in the world. Hence I value the opportunity to be alongside people in hospital. Here is a mobile community of folk aware of their deepest needs, willing to be real, and crying out to be heard and valued.

I know deep joy and deep pain as part and parcel of trusting in God and wrestling with him. This is not an easy faith or an easy gospel, but it is reality. God is for real: in the mess. And he makes something of it. Thank God. The course at Sarum nourished and changed me. What a rich, diverse group of people with diverse gifts and deep understanding and sensitivity. Thank you everyone. It was clear that, despite losses, each one IS using gifts. We received richly from one another. I long for others to receive from the insights of our weekend. There is much to offer those who are 'well'.

Gordon and Dot Squier

At about 30, I was a physics researcher working in Oxfordshire for the University of Birmingham. I was married to Dot who worked in the same establishment. We were both members of our local Methodist Church, where I became a Society Steward, Leader of a non-meeting Class, a member (and subsequently Chair) of the newly-emerged Neighbourhood Committee, and a helper at the Youth Club. I was becoming increasingly troubled by difficulty in walking any distance, besides other vague symptoms, and was eventually given the diagnosis of Multiple Sclerosis - on the day of the Church visit to see "Godspell"!

Early in 1976, when our eldest child was a few months old, a 'flare-up' of the MS put me in hospital just when I was preparing the Church Annual Report. Both staff and patients commented on the number of visitors I had, including fellow church members, (one a Local Preacher who was also an inpatient at the time,) besides work colleagues. Our son even encouraged an elderly lady whose enthusiasm for her daily walk round the ward was stimulated by the prospect of seeing 'the baby'! Going home two weeks later my mobility had been much improved, but I could no longer walk unaided. It was therefore no longer practicable for me to remain as Class Leader. My term as a Steward had also ended - but I could still assist at the Youth Club! The Department of Physics was very considerate while I was in hospital. It was decided to make my temporary appointment permanent, treating me as if I were still able-bodied.

In 1980 we moved to Birmingham, and through departmental connections we started going to Selly Oak Methodist Church. By this time I was more or less confined to a wheelchair outside the house, and it certainly saved on babysitters for our two youngsters to have the Class to which we were assigned meet at our house. Apart from membership of the Neighbourhood Committee for a while, I haven't held formal office at SOMC.

How has disability affected my faith? Having been brought up in a family where my mother progressively lost her sight, becoming totally blind in her mid-forties, I have been aware of disability as a fact of life, not seeing it as God's judgment. So I don't think my own disability has affected my faith negatively, but maybe made me more aware of the love of God. I feel one could experience the love of God through the hands of other people, not necessarily Christians, often in the little things, sometimes in major sacrifice, especially carers (and one in particular!) My aunt once asked whether I minded talking about MS, to which I replied, No, as long as it's not the only topic of conversation. Holidaying as a family at a centre for handicapped and able-bodied, as we have done for over 20 years, has provided a multitude of opportunities for doing other things than just talking about (or merely managing) one's own disability. The weekend at Sarum had many of the same features, with the major bonus of being approached within a significantly spiritual, rather than an (apparently) purely secular, context.

Carol Collier

My walk alongside those living with difficulty, difference and disability started as a child. I had near neighbours who were deaf and blind – yet raised a child and had a dog which was amazing to me as a 7 year old. My number one book, the first I purchased myself, whilst in primary school, was Helen Keller's, 'Teacher'. I never saw disability as a thing to be feared, rather my response was curiosity. Questions like, 'how could, what if, why?' never entered my mind. The first boy I, as a budding woman, 'noticed' had one leg shorter than the other from Polio I think. Through my teenage years a partially sighted peer was my closest friend and my favourite school teacher was a teacher who walked with sticks. He always had time to listen. I even married a man who suffered from depression. When after some years as a Christian I was struggling to serve God more fully it was the gift of the Deaf Community's language that helped me to 'hear' that the gospel was something to relate to, not reason with. The rhythm and movement of sign language woke up the passion for intimacy with God within me. I learned that the Christian life was a dance with God, not a mental agility exercise with the Scriptures.

My friendship with blind people taught me that if I could not 'see' my way then asking for help was not demeaning. Rather it was common sense, and saved hours of unnecessary loneliness and sometimes could be the start of a new friendship. Their daily life style humbled me. Living for over 20 years with family members who were depressed and shut me out of huge chunks of their lives drove me to find a deeper more intimate relationship with God. At one stage I wrote

"It feels like I am a fair damsel in the garden wearing a beautiful simple gown, my lover, (the depressed person) is wearing armour, and will not remove it as he approaches me. He insists on pressing against me, hurting me and pinching my soft flesh, but suddenly I realise it is Jesus who is pressing me to yield to Him, and when I do the joy is unspeakable."

My spiritual journey has found me deaf, blind and crippled in many ways. Reading, "knock and the door will be opened unto you" told me Jesus was not fazed by my disability – he had a ramp – it was His body on the cross – and He had put Himself at the door to open it up to me, if I would come. I have kept a journal for some twelve years detailing my disability and his provision. It is hard to condense all that into a couple of pages, but three years ago it became clear God had a personal mission for me to respond to if I would accept the invitation. It became the, 'Same Image – Different Package' project.

"The place where God calls you is the place where your deep gladness and the world's deep hunger meet." Frederick Buechner

This is my reality: I see the deep hunger of people who live with impairment and the deep loss of those who can't meet them on mutual ground. My deep delight is to bring them together.

Attending the Faith Journey of Impaired Pilgrims course in Sarum College in the spring was a refreshing interlude in a busy season for me. I met so many new and interesting people. Being able-bodied and without a caring role I could have felt quite out if it in this grouping of people, but although my disability may not be visible to others it is none the less very real. I felt totally at home. Also I had lots of opportunity to learn new angles on life with impairment, especially enduring physical pain. I was also thrilled that I had something to offer. Being familiar with a wide range of disability on a day to day basis I was able to help folk discover ways of including those with impairment that were unfamiliar to them such as passing around tactile objects, making sure speakers are not in front of light filled windows, and encouraging individuals to explain when they are being handicapped by another person's action, or inaction.

When we meet a person who is disabled, or has specific needs, we can often shy away feeling that we can't cope with their disability. Often it's because it meets us where our own disability or deep need is, and forces us to face up to it. As we'd rather not have it exposed, we tend to withdraw. When a disabled person meets an able bodied person, they too can shy away. Often it is because it meets them where their ability is hiding away, and they'd rather not have that exposed either because they'd have to take more responsibility. If we all hide our special need or our ability from each other, the treasure that God has placed in our beings fails to reach its full magnificence.

In our relationship with God it is the same. There is disability and ability on both sides. Unless we each acknowledge our situations and work together, both His and our magnificence is hindered from being revealed as it should be. Helen Keller said, "Life is a daring adventure or nothing at all." My mission, my daring adventure, is to bring to the church's attention the stunning treasure in those living with difficulty/difference/disability; to encourage them to experience God's enabling, healing and reconciliation through sharing their disability and ability with each other; and to do this across denominations, nations, age, race and impairment.

The principles that support my mission are sourced in the ways I read, see and experience the trinity approaching our impairment and disability: with deep compassion, earnest desire, unending curiosity about what might be, and appropriate challenge. The experiences that have substanced my mission are my personal experiences of being 'disabled' and 'dysfunctional', in many ways, and finding the trinity meeting me at every point of my impairment, very frequently through those who have had severe needs and disabilities themselves.

My involvement with the deaf, blind and mentally impaired has led me to discover more of my own 'impaired-ness,' and show me more and more of Father God's completeness. My involvement with the dying, mentally sick and housebound has taught me an untold number of lessons in humility, and dying to self, helping me become more like Jesus. My external and internal reconciliation and healing in these areas has enabled me to reach out with faith and courage to many who have had a variety of special needs/disabilities and offer them the same as the trinity has offered me.... And wow they have seen and accepted God's transformation in their lives too. So, with the Holy Spirit's guiding, my mission has been sustained and hopefully will be extended.

Helen Tyers: My journey with me (but did the church came along too?)

The journey to Sarum started a long time ago. It has been one that has had many bumps and hills but I would not have missed it for the world. I don't regret who I am or the bits that don't work. In fact they are to be celebrated as they have formed the essential me. This of course was not always how I felt. I have had those times of despair, times when the mind is so filled with pain that not a lot else can get in, the regrets that I cannot do certain things any longer. I can identify with the Christ on the cross shouting 'My God why have you left me?' Yet I can celebrate and identify with the Risen Christ that has passed through those dark days and, as He retained those marks, yet showed that there is a wounded wholeness to be had. He said, 'this is my body broken for you', I suppose the least I can do is to bring my broken body and place it at His service.

I was training to be a nurse when waking up one day I found I could not walk. It had been my dream for years to become a nurse and serve as a missionary in Kathmandu. After six weeks flat on my back I was able to return, but only for a short while, before the body gave out again. Clearly I was not going to be able to finish my training. I left nursing and after a few years, found work as a residential care officer for people with Autism.

This started me on a career in social work, moving to social services and child care, then into adult care. It was here I found my niche. My body continued to play me up, on and off, until the on was more than the off, and slowly but surely less of me worked in the way it had once done and the pain increased. I wanted so much to remain working: to be valuable and valued. So despite times when I could scarcely think for pain, I kept walking as much as I could. At work they were starting to comment on my health and safety and the risk of me falling, which was quite high. Then one day I was unable to do something with my boys, and going to the supermarket consisted of being draped over a trolley and dragged round. So I decided that using a wheelchair was the right thing to do. Work was still encouraging me to think of early retirement, but I was only in my early 30's and wanted to continue.

I love my wheelchairs; they are the best thing since sliced bread. With them I was free again, at least for a time. I could push myself and carry on with my life. I applied to go to university to become a qualified social worker. Having got my place, my employers took it off me, because I was a Disabled Person. For a few years prior to this I had become active in my union, fighting for Disabled People's rights. I have even been known to picket bus and train stations, taking care not to chain myself to anything in case it continued to move. So I should have been prepared for this to happen, but I was devastated. I fought hard, and took my employers to an industrial tribunal. They never saw the irony that they thought I would not be able to do it because I was a Disabled Person, yet due to their actions, I attended university on 'day release' worked with a full social work case load, and coped with the stress of grievance hearings and preparing for the tribunal. To cap it all they decided towards the end that actually I was not a Disabled Person under the DDA 1995 and therefore they did not have to 'answer' to me. So I was forced to have medical reports to show that I was. This was a key point for me. Up to that time I had had a number of different diagnoses, none of which had lasted for long before a bright eyed doctor came out with another answer and another theory.

This consultant was very clear that he could diagnose my condition. He wrote to my GP (who had started to tell me it was all in my mind) that my conditions were chronic and recognised. My employer gave in and 'settled out of court'. It was a small sum, but more importantly eight policy points were established so that no other Disabled Person would go through what I went through ever again at least in that authority. This battle has become vital to understanding where I am now with myself and with my God.

A short while after this I attended a Churches Together meeting in our town. I was greeted with, 'what shall we do with you?' An acquaintance passing by and saying hello was pounced on to take care of me which, knowing me, she refused to do. I was actually waiting for my husband to park the car. I asked for the words of the songs and was told I could not have them as they were on the OHP. I pointed out that I would not be able to see the OHP when everyone stood up, but they still refused. So we found a place to be on the end of a row, I collared the minister of that church and asked for the words, which he gave me. All was fine until one of the men then felt that I should move. Apparently I had become a fire hazard. I did point out to him that in the event of the building burning down I would be leaving it as quickly as anyone else, and that so far I had never spontaneously combusted, neither did I smoke, so I was not going to start one. I was told to 'go over there in the corner out the way'. At which point I went through the door and out of the church. Very angry and upset, after a little rage, I decided that this was not good enough. I would not accept being treated like that outside the church, so why should I allow the church to treat me like that?

This was the start of my theological reflection on what it means to be a Disabled Christian. I now have a masters degree in practical theology, and my journey from that day has strengthened my pride (in a good way) in who I am. I can be a valued child of God. I am made in God's image. I can identify with the wounded Christ, and I can be of service to Him. I have had many more occasions of hurt and exclusion. Apparently (so I was told) if I was really filled with the Holy Spirit 'it' would all go away, which was rather like my mothers solution. According to her, if I wore a vest I would not be a Disabled Person any more.

Not so long back I went to see my superintendent minister. I told him that I felt called to do some work, and thought I should seek ordination. My Minster asked me what I did now. I explained that I have maintained my campaigning in the wider world of social policy and I am on national task forces to change social work practice. I have written a book and now, in my spare time (I still work), I am acting as an expert witness in 6 court cases where Disabled People have had their children taken off them because they are Disabled. My Minister told me that ministers are two a penny, but there is only one me out there doing the work I am. I am already in ministry, I am working for God.

So there you have it. I am Helen: owner of a wonderful dog, Cherry, who helps me practically; the Stirling Moss of the wheelchair world in my 6 wheeled independent suspension reclining powered wheelchair; no longer able to shove myself (but power is much more fun) whizzing around for God. But did the church come too? Unfortunately not yet, but I am working on it.

Tim Macquiban

For Sarum College, this conference was a learning experience. We had never been faced with the presence of more than the occasional wheelchair or person with impairment. Now we had a group of twenty people with varying degrees of mobility, hearing and sight, ·pain and strength, staying for a whole weekend. We'd always prided ourselves on the quality of Sarum's hospitality. The newly installed lift allows greater access to all the different user groups who come into the college at the different levels of this historic Grade 1 listed building. But the real test was yet to come!

I guess for the duration of the conference there was a greater awareness of the need to be alert to how others were feeling, coping, as well as contributing in different ways, to our experience of engaging with difficult issues, not just for the churches we represented, but ourselves as feeling vulnerable individuals who come with all manner of impairments, physical, mental and spiritual. I expected that it might be difficult, not least because my own level of impairment (hearing) is not severe and I have never known any different.

What was most amazing for me was how well everyone got on and formed a new community. Yes – the body of Christ in all its brokenness. And yet with a "lively hope of resurrection", here and now, as signs of new life were discovered, recognized, shared. Signs sometimes buried or ignored by our churches but too powerful to be contained within the grave of our disappointments, frustrations and sense of falling short of what others would have us be.

And this was a model for Sarum College as an institution. Fragile, vulnerable, falling short often of its aspirations, weakened by the strength of powerful competitors yet fiercely independent with a mission to succeed whatever the odds. And our new sense of what it means to be open to all has been enriched by our hosting of the weekend and all that it gave us, as individuals and as an institution. This publication is one with which we are proud to be associated and hope that it will be a fitting tool for further explorations with a wider group of people in faith communities and beyond.

Mary Grey

The whole experience at Sarum College was for me strange, unexpected and only in retrospect, grace-filled. When I was initially approached by Donald, Peter and Tim I was enthusiastic about the project, because I thought it was important and could form a vital part of Sarum College's mission. I thought it also a seriously neglected area of Liberation Theology, but I did not think of the area of disability as something that touched me personally. But almost immediately something strange happened. An intermittent back problem over the last 30 years suddenly reappeared and showed every intention of having come to stay. I began the weary round of X-rays, back pain clinics, ineffective pain killers, Alexander Technique and Chiropractics, only to be told firmly that I would have to learn to live with this condition and that the pain would never go.

So, what had begun as a journey of solidarity with impaired pilgrims took on a more personal meaning. I could no longer speak in objective terms, even if I ever should have done so in the first place!

What happened that weekend at Sarum took place on two levels. Firstly, I was part of the team and so partly responsible for the smooth running of the weekend. I was also a speaker. Yes, I believed everything I had prepared in my talk – only now I was saying it with a far more involved "I" or "we" than I had imagined. But secondly, on another level, I was learning and being challenged about the spiritual journey – by everyone I met. This was a very uncomfortable process, not least because of being in a position of responsibility without much time for personal reflection.

Fellow journeyers challenged me in their level of courage and ability to be joyful and convey a great sense of energy and determination, despite all the difficulties and restrictions of their lives. But the need to re-think basic principles of faith was the deepest challenge. I had been trying to live an activist version of Christianity all my life, convinced that "feeding the hungry", "giving water to the least of the little ones", and so on, was the bedrock of faith. Now I was part of a group of believers living out of deep faith, and yet who were challenging me to a different expression. Feminist theology and spirituality had already privileged embodied faith, but I still think there was a presumption of an able body behind this. Indeed all the notions of wholeness and well-being are still resting on the basis of this "able body", or nearest approximation. I now understand that there are many varieties of "wholeness", just as there are with healing. I am also convinced that what we were articulating at Sarum is important far beyond this small group: the reality of being an "impaired pilgrim" is for all believers.

So I am grateful to participants of the weekend for inverting the stereotypes, for showing me that the greatest need is not to be helped but to be empowered to share one's own giftedness. And my fellow pilgrims gave me one of the most moving gifts of my own life: my own Church forbids the ordination of women yet the community this weekend invited me to lead the Eucharistic prayer, specially written for the occasion by Peter Cole. I will never stop being grateful for this, and for that experience which brought us all very close. It was a closure of the weekend experience, but a first step on the next part of the journey.

70

Kerstin and Donald Eadie

'Don't grieve for what you can no longer do – enjoy and explore what you can.'

We moved to Birmingham in 1987. Kerstin first worked at the Selly Oak Colleges teaching Namibians preparing to use English as a medium in education. Later she became head of the language development base at the Selly Park School for girls. Donald is a Methodist Minister and served as Chairman of the Birmingham District of the Methodist Church until 1996. Due to a developing degenerative disc disease in the spine he had to take early retirement. Three major operations have been necessary including the implanting of scaffolding. He continues to live with pain.

We offer glimpses into our shared journey as one way of understanding the wider conversation which is always necessary in a household composed of someone living with impairment and a carer.

The roots of Kerstin's family reach back into the 17th century and are in Nås, a village in the forests of central Sweden. Each summer we, and others, return there like migrating birds. This is a significant journey in itself. Nor is it easy to leave. This year we chose not to drive directly to the ferry in Gothenburg but to travel via the scenic route along the west coast. Before going to university Kerstin had worked in a mental hospital in Uddevalla and has dreamed of returning and sharing with Donald the beauty of that coastal area. The journey was wonderful in many ways and will be savoured in the years to come.

The journey was yet another learning experience for both of us. Donald has a serious spinal condition and this limits his ability to walk and to sit. We therefore had to discover new strategies for living within unfamiliar contexts.

71

What was the nature of this learning? Well, at one level we had to work with practical things: Finding parking for the car close by the Vandrarhem so that Kerstin could move the special chair and luggage easily, for there was no disabled parking. (A Vandrarhem is a comfortable modestly priced hostel for both young and old.) How firm are the beds and if they are bunk beds who sleeps on the top and who the bottom? And finding a place to eat with convenient parking in busy little seaside towns? And would the small restaurant receive a large chair? And managing the indoor and outdoor museum in Vitlycka and the search for a flat and shaded piece of lawn to stretch out the blanket and to lay down the pillow. And within these days when and where to build in the rest times? And at night there where conflicting needs: the one relaxing and reading, the other wanting 'the holding and the being held.'

We constantly make choices about possibilities. What to do together and what separately? How to live both positively and realistically? What 'to have a go at' knowing that it could be great, even memorable, but also knowing that Donald may have to pay for it physically later and that Kerstin may have to forgo parts of a desired adventure? And at times we get things wrong, we become over tired, anxious and irritable. And at other times we manage better than we could have hoped. And within the practicality of daily management and the search for effective strategies there lie deeper questions:

What does it mean to love within all these tiresome realities, to keep on and on being mindful and aware of the needs of the other, to seek their good, and at the same time, honestly and openly, to listen to our own heart's desire, to acknowledge our own needs?

And what of our journey into becoming more human women and men, still learning to live with our changing bodies, our sexuality, our spirituality, our nature?

And the journey into acceptance? What is to be accepted and what confronted?

And the carers, the spouses? Can our needs also be taken seriously, our faith journeys also receive attention, affirmation and nurture?

We have found Peter Millar's prayer helpful.

Lord of every pilgrim heart,
bless our journeys
on these roads
we never planned to take
but
through your
surprising wisdom
discovered
we were
on.

Peter Cole

I am writing this sitting in a folding chair beside the sea. It is a pebble beach, so the waves are making that wonderful swishing, grinding noise as they push in and pull back. I grew up beside the sea. I walked my dog along the shoreline every morning, swam in its waters during the summer, and learnt to catch its fish. Then we moved inland. First to Bristol where I trained for the Methodist ministry, and then into the Midlands for my first and second circuit appointments. Here we were about as far from the coast as you could get. The air was different: hot, still, heavy, lifeless. The only swimming available was in a chlorinated pool, but still I went regularly. It helped, a little. Then, when I had to retire from the ministry on health grounds, we eventually returned, back to the sea. You could say the sea has been pain's gift back to me, a sort of recompense for all it has taken away. A fair trade? I'm not sure, see what you think.

I was a fit, healthy, active young man. I walked every morning, swam, played various sports, cycled and ran regularly. Then, while we were in Bristol, I began getting pain in my right hip and leg. After various treatments it went away, only to return a few years later, stronger and more debilitating. This time treatment did not reduce it. A back operation which promised complete relief only made things much worse. Eventually I was told I would have to learn to live with it. At this time I was receiving support from my circuit superintendent and chairman of the district. They encouraged me to see that, "learning to live with it", could not include carrying on in active ministry. I was forced to retire on health grounds aged only 39 years. Suddenly the support I had previously received disappeared.

At the time I was two thirds of the way through a master's degree in applied theology at Westminster College, Oxford. I chose to research the pastoral care offered to people in chronic pain as my dissertation subject. I interviewed around twenty people and again and again I heard the same story, a story which I too was now living. The church did not know what to do with people who struggled with pain every day. Our stories were a combination of courage and despair in the face of loss and exclusion. Our lives were a living challenge to an easy theology of God's love and power. Our faith journeys were frequently travelled through darkness and unknowing. We found ourselves in an uneasy existence on the boundaries and edges of the church and of faith. And there was seldom anywhere where we could share these stories and feel that we had been heard and understood.

In my own attempt to make sense of my pain-full faith journey I have found myself travelling further and further away from the traditions of theology and doctrine. There have been many fellow travellers who have helped me to search for a new path. Some of these where feminist theologians. As I am a man this might surprise you but it was in their writings that I found a willingness to deconstruct our models of God and to revalue the place of the body and creation in our theologies. As I read women who were attempting to do theology from the basis of their own, previously excluded, experience I recognised the value of their work for my own context. With them I found increasingly meaningless the all-powerful Father God presented through most worship and theology. I joined a feminist liturgy group and through our creative worship, silences, circle dances, and liturgical actions that embraced the body and the earth, I began to glimpse the possibility of God again.

There is an irony here! When you are in continuous pain you can learn to hate your own body. It becomes your own personal torturer: on hand at every moment to twist the knife. And yet of course you cannot escape it, and any theology which ignores our physical context and the suffering which so often accompanies it becomes worthless. Only those who are willing to acknowledge the way our experience of our bodies shapes our theologies and our understanding of God can truly speak to those who live the story of pain.

Feminist theology also draws attention to those who are excluded from our traditions: those whose narratives are not reflected in our language, symbols and prayers; whose experiences are devalued as threatening or dangerous. Here again I found points of connection with my own experience and with those whose stories I had heard. It was not uncommon for us to be told that somehow our failure to be cured of pain was our own fault. That which was central to our existence was denied value. Our pain made us somehow dirty or unfaithful. We became a threat to faith, best ignored or silenced. The process used by feminist theologians offered hope. It suggested that, on the contrary, it was precisely within the lives of those who were marginalised and excluded from the traditional narrative that the God of vulnerability became known. Perhaps our stories of pain could become incarnational?

This is a journey which continues and following it has not exactly made my relationship with the established church easy. Sitting through most traditional worship is now, shall we say, 'challenging'! It is a painful experience in more ways than one because I cannot any more bring myself to worship the God that I usually find presented there. And there is still the anger and bitterness that I must watch others do that from which I am now excluded. So I have had to turn to other sources of inspiration: the liturgy group I mentioned, Sarum College, occasional visits to Quaker Meeting, the valued support of close friends, and of course the sea.

I walk along the shoreline every morning. Sometimes when the pain is bad this is slow, halting and brief. At other times the rhythm of walking helps to loosen up stiff muscles. I often stop and sit on the pebbles and just watch the waves. The sea is never the same: she is a living breathing uncertainty that challenges our desire for order and shape. She offers herself to my whole body through every sense. In the summer she bears that body and for a moment carries its pain. She encourages reflection, and joy. At times she can be terrifying. She speaks to me of God.

This is good because at this point in my journey God seems to slip through my fingers like sea water cupped in the hand. I have lost so much and it is hard to forgive God for that. But I have to acknowledge that my pain has shaped me into the person I now am. What small inner strength I have is partly the gift of struggling with pain's burden. My theology and belief also owe their shape to this struggle. Pain has brought me into contact with many wonderful people. It has helped me to stop, and offered me the gift of time in which to read and think. It gave me the chance to care for my children and support my wife in her developing career. And, as I have said, it brought me back to the sea. All of these are pain's gift to me. But alongside them I have to place so much: despair, loss, grief, darkness, and (lest this be forgotten) the desire in every moment that the pain should just, simply, GO.

Well, I have sat for long enough. Not even the sight of those waves crashing onto the shore and the taste of the spray are enough to offset the discomfort I now feel. Everything these days has to be taken in small doses. But I will be back, and I know that she will be waiting for me: ready to welcome me, to share her beauty, to receive whatever I need to tell her, and to speak to me gently of the mystery of God. May the blessing of her white waves be with me, and with you.

CPSIA information can be obtained at www.ICGtesting.com
Printed in the USA
BVOW05s1710170214

345174BV00018B/1039/P